THE PERFECT CHILD

At school, in the 1960s, David Gold was considered the "teacher's pet." At college, David became a highly successful psychology major and graduated cum laude.

He attended his sister Sally's wedding, serving as best man. In characteristic fashion, he was considerate of and cooperative with all who were present. Three weeks later, to the shock of everyone who knew him, twenty-three-year-old David bought a gun, went home, and shot and killed his father. Then he shot and killed his mother. Finally, he shot and killed himself.

A note was found where the murders and suicide took place in his parents' bedroom. The note read, "I've been trying too hard."

"Revealing . . . A noteworthy study . . . Analyzes murder within families, serial killing and suicide, and concludes by showing how we can understand and overcome the murder 'in our hearts.' "

Publishers Weekly

OUR WISH TO KILL

THE MURDER IN ALL OUR HEARTS

DR. HERBERT S. STREAN
AND LUCY FREEMAN

AVON BOOKS ◆ NEW YORK

AVON BOOKS
A division of
The Hearst Corporation
1350 Avenue of the Americas
New York, New York 10019

The St. Martin's Press edition contains the following Library of Congress Cataloging in Publication Data:

Strean, Herbert S.
  Our wish to kill: the murder in all our hearts / Herbert Strean and Lucy Freeman.
    p.   cm.
  1. Murder—United States—Psychological aspects. I. Title
HV6529. S77 1991   90-48346
616.89—dc20   CIP

First Avon Books Printing: April 1993

AVON TRADEMARK REG. U.S. PAT. OFF. AND IN OTHER COUNTRIES, MARCA REGISTRADA, HECHO EN U.S.A.

Printed in the U.S.A.

RA 10 9 8 7 6 5 4 3 2 1

Contents

Acknowledgments

First and foremost we wish to thank Robert Weil, Senior Editor, for his sensitive editing, valuable suggestions, and genuine appreciation of human conflict. His enthusiasm has been most gratifying to both of us and we value him as friend and colleague. We also want to thank Bill Thomas, associate editor, Richard Romano, editorial assistant, and John Murphy, our inspired publicist, for their helpful contributions.

Our profound gratitude goes to Jane Dystel, our literary agent, who always helps us see the dimensions involved in writing a book. Her perceptiveness and awareness of what a reader values most is much appreciated.

We are grateful to both Paul Moor and Sylvia Honig for allowing us to quote from their books. Mr. Moor has given us permission to use material from *The Self-Portrait of Jürgen Bartsche* and Ms. Honig from *Born to Kill*, a book she is writing on the life of Willie James Bosket, Jr. We also thank Myra MacPherson for allowing us to quote from her illuminating article on the life of Theodore Bundy, which appeared in the May 1989 issue of *Vanity Fair.*

Finally we wish to thank Marcia Strean, who constantly devotes much time and attention to being the authors' favorite critic.

We thank each other for mutual pleasure in producing our sixth book without one overt sign of wishing to murder each other!

Herbert S. Strean
Lucy Freeman
November 1990

And he was rich—yes, richer than a king—
  And admirably schooled in every grace:
In fine, we thought that he was everything
  To make us wish that we were in his place.

So on we worked, and waited for the light,
  And went without the meat, and cursed the bread;
And Richard Cory, one calm summer night,
  Went home and put a bullet through his head.

—EDWARD ARLINGTON ROBINSON
"Richard Cory"

Prologue

In this book, our main objective is to show that the difference between the overt murderer, such as a Theodore Bundy, and the rest of us is only a matter of degree. We also would like to demonstrate that all children and all parents hold murderous wishes toward each other, and to reveal how these early murderous wishes toward parents, siblings, and others become reenacted in later relationships in love, marriage, child-rearing, and work.

While the difference is a matter of degree, what produces that "degree" is the subject of this book. Why are so many of us able to handle our murderous feelings, while others are driven to carry them out and destroy children or adults whom they may not even know?

Not only are we interested in shedding light on the murder in our hearts but also in exploring why we often direct our murderous wishes toward ourselves. Just as we can demean, derogate, and psychologically destroy one another, we are all capable of suicide and can become so depressed, masochistic, and self-torturing that we put an end to our own lives.

It is our conviction that the murder in all our hearts can be tamed and overt violence diminished. We will show how we can become more loving, constructive human beings so that the hate-filled part of our culture may be turned into a more thoughtful, caring society.

PART 1

Our Need to Murder

1

Murder in the Air

Asked if she ever felt the wish to kill, Alice Donenfeld, prominent attorney and entrepreneur in the international entertainment business, laughingly replied, "You mean how many times a day?"

Joseph Kallinger, born in Philadelphia on December 11, 1936, was a healthy, full-term baby, a "grand" baby as his mother described him. She hated to part with him, yet wished to be free of him. From day one, she was unsure whether she wanted to keep him or get rid of him—an agonizing conflict.

Joseph's mother had married at nineteen, given birth to a daughter in September 1935, then left her husband three months later. While separated from her husband, planning to divorce him, she engaged in an affair with a man identified only as T., as the late Flora Rheta Schreiber relayed the story in her book *The Shoemaker*. After Joseph's mother informed T. she was pregnant, he walked out of her life.

For one month following Joseph's birth, his mother breast-fed him, played with him lovingly, sang to him, cuddled him. She was later to say, "I gave him everything because I knew he wouldn't have it for long."

When the month ended, she suddenly turned him over to the care of strangers in a private boarding home. Three months later he was taken to an orphanage where he remained for twenty-two months. At this time, his mother resumed her affair with T. She told him of the birth of their son, and pleaded to get married. He revealed something he had neglected to tell her—that he was already married and had several children he did not wish to leave.

Joseph's mother then gave up hope of providing her son a home with her and his father. She had been reluctant to put him up for adoption but then did. On October 25, 1938, at the age of twenty-two months, able to walk and to talk, Joseph left the orphanage for a trial preview at the home of Stephen and Anna Kallinger. If this proved successful, the couple planned to adopt him.

The Kallingers were in their early forties and childless. Stephen had proved sterile, and they wanted a son who would become a shoemaker and inherit their prospering shoe repair business, as well as take care of them in their old age. As Joseph grew up, they constantly reminded him that *they* had rescued him from an orphanage, that he *owed* them everything he ate, wore, and possessed. At the slightest infraction of their rigid rules, they threatened to return him to the orphanage.

By the age of six, Joseph clearly felt like an intruder in the house. He wondered when he would be thrown out, as he later told Schreiber. His self-doubts, his constant fear of abandonment—the most devastating fear a child can have—and his lack of self-esteem, all increased at six and a half when he had to undergo an operation for a hernia. In the hospital, he fantasied that the Kallingers had sent him back to the orphanage as they so frequently threatened.

Lying on his hospital bed he was obsessed with thoughts of steel knives. Anna had told him a knife would be used on him during the operation. Joseph had seen knives in the shoe repair shop. They were to become for him instruments of power and authority through which those giants called "grown-ups" enforced their will by cutting leather or a little boy's flesh if he was "bad."

Following the hernia operation, the Kallingers told Joseph a "demon" had lived in his "bird," their word for penis, and the doctor had driven out the demon by operating on his penis, making it smaller so it would never grow. Therefore, Joseph would never get into trouble, because a bird without its demon could never get hard. The Kallingers were clearly very emotionally disturbed people who feared their own sexual impulses.

While the "bird" myth was no doubt one of the major psychological abuses inflicted on Joseph, there were many others. Anna led him to and from school until he was thirteen, infantilizing him at a time he should have been encouraged to be on his own. She also isolated him from all playmates. When his schoolmates attacked him and he did not fight back, she called him "chicken" and "yellow."

The Kallingers kept him virtually chained to the shoe repair store. After school and weekends he was never allowed to play with other children or bring them to his home, but forced to work in the shop with his father. He lived completely in a world of his own.

He was also cruelly physically abused. If he disobeyed in any way, he was forced to kneel on his bare knees on a strip of coarse sandpaper used in the shop for sanding leather. He often knelt for an hour or longer until one of the Kallingers told him he could get up. For a minor provocation, they burned the tips of his fingers on a gas stove. One day when he was ten he asked to visit the zoo with his class, and Anna hit him over the head with a hammer because he pleaded that his father had told him he could go. Stephen then openly flogged the boy with two thick shoe soles placed together, beating him on his nude back, arms, legs, and head, as he did when Joseph disobeyed.

At the age of twelve Joseph cut a hole in his bedroom wall, and, as he told Schreiber, after masturbating in the hole he would use a knife to stab the breasts in photographs of nude women, an action that made him feel strong. At fifteen, achieving the fullest intensity of his sexuality, Joseph's head would jerk from side to side and his body would writhe as he masturbated. He frequently laughed uncontrollably and without provocation, as if life were a terrifying joke.

At this time the Kallingers started to be afraid of him, and placed a lock on their bedroom door. When he wanted to know why they did this, they told him, "There are changes in you we don't like." To their relief, Joseph asked if he could rent a furnished room nearby, and moved out of the Kallinger home but continued to work in the shoe repair shop.

At sixteen he left school to marry a girl he thought he loved, and they had two children. Shortly thereafter, she ran off with another man and divorced Kallinger, leaving their son and daughter for him to bring up. He then married a young woman named Betty, and they eventually had three more children. On the surface Joseph seemed a conscientious parent who loved his children and was a good provider as he became a successful shoemaker.

One day, fearing that his second wife would also leave him (who could possibly love a "bad boy"?), he dug a deep hole in the earth under the shoe repair shop as a hiding place to protect himself. While sitting in the hole he began to hear voices that told him to hurt and murder people.

Thus began a series of cruel, mad, murderous acts including the use of a hot spatula in 1972, when he was thirty-six, to burn his thirteen-year old daughter's thigh because she was late coming home the previous night. He warned, "You will never run away from me again." He was replaying the anguish he had never ceased to feel at the cruelty of his foster mother when she burned his hands if he threatened to leave her. We often act out in later life the exact cruelties that have been inflicted on us as children.

Two years later Kallinger became determined to destroy the world. He wanted to kill every man, woman, and child on the face of the earth, saying "God" instructed him to do so. Between 1972 and 1974 he committed three murders.

On July 7, 1974, he and his son Michael killed an eleven-year-old Philadelphia youth, José Collageo, a victim picked at random from a city playground. Two weeks later Kallinger murdered his own son Joey, fourteen, by tying him to a ladder and drowning him in a stagnant pool of water at a construction site. On January 8, 1975, he and Michael broke into a home in Leonia, New Jersey, and murdered Maria Fasching, a nurse visiting there. While she lay dying, one of the hostages Kallinger had taken managed to escape and went for help. Kallinger and his son fled, but he left his bloody shirt, with his initials on it, in a pool nearby and the police arrested him eleven days later.

As Schreiber interviewed Joseph in prison and learned of the terror in his life, she realized the pain of his early days and how his mind had been affected by the foster parents' cruelties. She understood that he had never received love from anyone, but had been treated with a hatred and contempt that had made him schizophrenic.

After her account of Kallinger's life, *The Shoemaker,* was published following the appearance of her popular book *Sybil,* Schreiber often visited Joseph. She told Lucy Freeman, her close friend, "I feel like the mother he never had." She talked to Joseph almost daily on the telephone, paying all the bills, until the day she died in November 1988.

Joseph recently told Freeman on the telephone, "We had a relationship that no real son or mother on this planet ever had. We filled each other's emotional needs. It's just not the same since Flora died." Flora had yearned for a son and Joseph was desperately in need of a loving mother.

Since Schreiber's death from cancer, Joseph has threatened repeatedly to kill himself by not eating. The latest attempt, as this book was being written, was in the summer of 1990. Kallinger, who over the years had sometimes spoken to Freeman on the phone when she visited Flora, sent

Freeman a letter on August 3, 1990, saying he was on a hunger strike and intended to die from starvation.

He wrote her, "I want to be as close to Flora as possible at my end now. She not only shared her life with me as my mother and I as her son but also shared her close friends with me of which you are one."

He added that on Father's Day he had been all alone. None of his four children had "cared to even write me a card and in between hallucinations like movie pictures I saw Heads soaked in blood."

He also enclosed an article written by Bill Sanderson, staff writer for *The Record* in Waymart, Pennsylvania, which described how Kallinger, now in the Farview State Hospital, a mental hospital for the criminally insane in the Poconos, had refused to eat. Sanderson quoted Kallinger as saying he had a right to die yet was being force-fed.

Sanderson revealed that Schreiber had left Kallinger about $40,000 in her will. He told Sanderson, "She had no children, no family. I was it. She was trying to fill what my mother never gave to me and my adopted mother never gave me. I was the last thing on her breath in the hospital when she died."

Kallinger was part of a program on WOR television on August 17, 1990, titled "Should Convicted Killers Have the Right to Choose to Die?" He was interviewed in a question-and-answer format over the phone from Farview. A court order had ruled that he had to be fed through a tube in the nose, which Kallinger said was very painful. He was asked if he believed he had the right to starve to death. He replied, "God wants me to come home. Once He told me I was to destroy mankind through sexual destruction. I live with my guilt every day for the three murders. And, if I were let out of prison, I would kill again. I don't know how to stop. I get no help here. I see a psychiatrist for three minutes every Friday. That's not therapy."

He said he had known since the age of twelve every day of his life that he "would end in destroying others and then being destroyed." He added that when Schreiber was alive, she had pleaded for help for him because he was psychotic, and he had received that help at Farview for a number of years, but that today he lacked it and did not want to continue living. Steve Latimer, a lawyer on the program, described Kallinger's self-starvation as "a cry for help out of desperation as he pleads, 'Do something for me!' "

The life of Joseph Kallinger poignantly shows us why a human being may be driven to commit murder. The earlier in life a child experiences hatred and lack of love from those who supposedly care for him, the more likely the child is to become a potential murderer. Just as we know that the infant who receives tender love and care will emerge in all probability as a warm, giving person who trusts others, the infant who feels unloved, not given to, not cared for, is inexorably driven to do unto others what was done unto him.

What does it mean when we say parents must "love" a child, be able to nurture him, show him tenderness, care about him? It means not one but many things. It means, first of all, that both the mother and father want the child and do not deeply resent the idea of his conception.

It means that the prospective parents should be able to enjoy the pregnancy and look forward to the tasks ahead, such as feeding the baby, diapering him, soothing him when he is in pain, and gurgling and laughing with him when he wants to gurgle and laugh.

It means that both mother and father must treat the baby gently, not toss him about wildly or hurt him by pressing him too closely. It means that the mother and father can truly share the baby and at the same time respect and enjoy each other's unique relationship with the child. The father must be able to give up some of the attention he previously received from his wife while the mother cuddles the baby. The mother must be able to do the same—that is, adapt to receiving less attention from her husband while he frolics with the baby.

It means that the mother and father must never strike the baby or punish him severely if he disobeys. Instead, the baby should be comforted if he screams, not deprived of such essentials as food or sleep.

It means that the mother and father must be able to communicate with the child, be interested in his physical and mental growth, and help him gently to understand the difference between reasonable behavior and behavior that would hurt himself or others.

But what about parents who don't enjoy being parents? It is our strong conviction that one of the major causes of murder and other forms of violence is the child's realization that his parents are openly unhappy at being responsible for him. He interprets his parents' lack of pleasure in him as a signal that he is unlovable. Any child who feels he is not loved will be filled with hatred and may express it in a variety of ways, including overt murder.

Therefore, parents who do not enjoy their parenthood need help to overcome the obstacles within themselves that keep them from deriving joy from parenthood. We might compare the plight of parents who lack such pleasure in their children to that of men and women who don't derive pleasure from sex. Both groups need either therapeutic help or some form of counseling so that they can enjoy feelings that are meant to be enjoyed.

Some day our society will view the lack of pleasure in being a parent as a serious emotional problem that needs immediate attention, much like many medical problems. There is no doubt that the seeds of murder are planted in an atmosphere where parents are unhappy being parents.

The foster parents of Joseph Kallinger were unable to enjoy being parents. Instead they brutalized the child. The clear lesson we learn from his life is that all human beings relate to the world in the way their early world—parents and others who were close—related to them. Kallinger received tender love and care from his mother for only one month before she gave him to an orphanage, and his life thereafter showed the results of a lack of care—results that included a murderous feeling toward his own children.

Kallinger had been hated, abandoned, treated cruelly—hurt physically and emotionally by his supposed caretakers. His wish to kill, get revenge for their many constant cruelties, later erupted on innocent strangers. So intense was his rage, he wanted to get rid of the whole world, as he felt the Kallingers wanted to kill him.

How a child is treated early in life determines in many ways who will murder and who will not. This was clearly appreciated by our Biblical forefathers who talked about "an eye for an eye," and "a tooth for a tooth." These feelings translate into "If you hurt me or reject me, I will want to do the same to you."

Asked if she ever felt the wish to kill, Alice Donenfeld, prominent attorney and entrepreneur in the international entertainment business, laughingly replied, "You mean how many times a day?" Her father died when she was only twelve and she no doubt felt, in addition to grief, a natural feeling of abandonment. The more we feel unloved and abandoned as children, the more we are stirred by anger. To some degree, we all feel abandoned and unloved, for our childhood demands are often unreal. The actual murderer is so deeply deprived early in life that he felt little if any love from parents.

It should not be difficult to understand, even empathize with, a murderer when we look at his loveless childhood. Whether we know it or not, acknowledge it or not, whenever we feel unloved, rejected, threatened by the possible loss of someone we need desperately, we will feel intense rage. The more desperate our need for love and the more vulnerable we feel, the more we will hate. Since none of us can feel loved all the time, all of us are potential murderers. As Robert Weil, an editor, eloquently put it, "We all skate on a coating of mental ice."

Whether we become an overt murderer or merely murder in fantasy, the wish to kill originates from fallen self-esteem. We feel unappreciated, and in response to feeling slighted, we need to show in some fashion our fury at the hurt inflicted. We say to the offender, "You cannot do this to me without my hitting back when you do not appreciate me."

Joseph's childhood with the Kallingers falls into two parts—before and after his hernia operation at the age of six. *Before* was a time of compensating through fantasy for the feeling of not being "a part of anybody." *After* was a time of expressing through anger his reaction to the emotional deprivation and traumas the Kallingers inflicted.

Had he not brought a consuming rage to the Kallinger household when he was twenty-two months old and fresh from the orphanage, he still would have been vulnerable to and suffered from the Kallingers' cruel abuse. The anger he carried with him made him even more vulnerable.

If we look at Joseph's early life, we see clearly the reasons for his later murder of others who, in some way, reminded him of his unbelievably cruel foster parents. It is not by accident he killed Maria Fasching, the nurse in Leonia. She said "no" to him when he asked her to bite off the penis of a stranger he had stripped naked and tied to the floor of the cellar, intending to kill him. Joseph related to a "no" as if it came from the strict, hateful, cruel mother substitute who had brought him up. He then had been too small to wreak vengeance on her—he depended on her for his very existence. But as a man, with the boy's hatred boiling within, he felt more powerful at long last than the woman who at times had almost butchered him in his youth.

Joseph's infantile rage was spawned when he lost the "paradise" of infancy, separated forever at the age of one month from his mother. Because no loving mother immediately replaced his own, the separation instilled in him a deep anxiety at any kind of separation or loss of closeness. His murderous wishes were inevitable. He was driven to do unto others what had been done unto him. We may venture the guess that Cain, the world's first known murderer, felt as weak and vulnerable as Joseph Kallinger.

2

Why We Wish to Kill

Committing murder does not make murderous feelings disappear.

We read daily about the son or daughter, husband or wife who seems at least superficially to be a decent human being, goes to work and apparently is just like most of us. Then one day, to the shock of all who know him, he commits the brutal murder of a parent or sister or brother or mate or child or stranger.

Such a person makes us view murder as a mystery—as if his motives were difficult, if not impossible, to fathom. Yet if the life story of a seemingly nonprovocative, unobtrusive, possibly even outwardly kind person is examined, we may discover the murderous fantasies he has harbored over the years. He usually has turned those fantasies against himself in the form of depression (the burying from consciousness of the wish to kill), extreme self-hatred, or possibly even schizophrenia, until one day they erupt in murder.

We should keep in mind that, although men or women supposedly above reproach "suddenly" commit murder, as children they felt deprived, misunderstood, abused, hated, and yearned for the love of parents unable to give it because of their own tortured lives as children.

To keep the hope for love alive, most children prefer to feel like "bad" boys and "bad" girls and turn their hatred on themselves rather than show the slightest sign of defying their parents.

Parents frequently give mixed or "double-bind" messages to children. One message is of love, the other of hate. The mother who admonishes her child as he goes off to school, "Be careful you don't fall down, smash your arms and break your teeth!" is saying, unconsciously, I wish you would do all this, you troublesome child, and then I would be free of you.

No one of us as yet born can love consistently. The saint has not yet appeared in the realm of parenthood. Yet it is an axiom that when a child is loved, he feels good; when hated, he feels bad. All of us would rather love and be loved than hate and be hated.

When we feel misunderstood, deprived, hated, we try to control our rage and somehow restore a loving relationship. It is only after we have tried time and time again as a child to love and be loved, and failed, that as an adult we give in to murderous wishes and feelings.

The wish to murder can never be divorced from the setting in which the actual murderer or the one fantasying murder finds himself. There is all the difference in the world between a soldier killing an enemy in a sanctioned war and a husband who lives in an upper middle-class suburb smashing his wife in the face or murdering her out of hatred.

In the first case the culture rewards the soldier, makes him a hero, gives him medals, honors him. In the second case, the culture forbids a husband to abuse his wife physically. If he does, he is labeled "cruel" and a "coward."

But there is great variation, even among middle-class married couples, as to how to cope with blows to the body and the lessening of self-esteem that follows. Two decades ago in a fashionable suburban Connecticut community, a Congressman was brought to court for violently striking his wife during an argument.

The wife told the judge, "Your Honor, in Polish families, which I come from, this is the way we resolve conflict. My husband and I really love each other. Otherwise we wouldn't have stayed together all these years."

Neighbors had brought the case to court because they could not tolerate the wife's constant shrieks of pain. She, however, stoically accepted her pain as the way to "resolve conflict," not as a sign of her husband's brutality and her masochistic willingness to be regularly beaten.

In trying to understand murderous fantasies and deeds, we always have to keep in mind the setting in which murder takes place. In some cultures, ethnic groups, and families, hate and murderous fantasies expressed to some degree, either physically or in sarcastic words that tear the other person apart emotionally, are quite sanctioned, even championed. In other families, neighborhoods, and cultures, even to harbor a hostile thought is considered a mortal sin.

Committing murder does not make murderous feelings disappear. They still exist and will continue to be strong until the emotional roots that fashioned them are unearthed and faced. Unless the murderer understands why he murdered—which means an investigation into his background (that inevitably turns out to be a childhood surfeited with cruelty on the part of parents, mental or physical or both) his murderous feelings will not be alleviated and he may be tempted to kill again.

As we examine cultures where large numbers of overt murders take place frequently, such as in the black neighborhoods of our large cities, certain characteristics of the hate culture emerge. What are these characteristics?

Poverty is chief among them, with a lack of food and other basic essentials. Those who live in these areas feel little self-esteem and are full of hatred toward those who can live more comfortably and peacefully. The more such human needs as food, clothing, and adequate shelter are lacking, the higher the incidence of murder.

In our country, at least half the dozens of murders a day are perpetrated by members of minority groups, especially in this era of crack and cocaine. When someone feels deprived and neglected, he is far more inclined to hate. A culture that breeds poverty and deprivation will create murderous men, women, and children.

Long before the social sciences evolved and long before psychoanalysis was a gleam in Freud's eye, writers and artists were aware of how poverty could lead to murder. This is dramatically illustrated in fiction by Charles Dickens, and by Dostoyevski in *Crime and Punishment,* where the dreams of the main character, Raskolnikov, who commits murder, abound with scenes of animals and innocent people being beaten.

There has hardly been an attack more vicious than that of a group of young blacks and Hispanics from Harlem out on a "wilding" spree as they invaded the northern area of Central Park one dark night in the summer of 1989. They brutally attacked a young white woman running for exercise around the reservoir. They left her bloody and ostensibly dead after sexually abusing her in the bushes, smashing her head open.

This was not exclusively a sexual act. With rape, there occurs simultaneously a vicious level of violence. That she was saved by an expert medical team proved a miracle and a testament to her strong will to live. Most of the blood had drained from her body, affecting her brain, before she was discovered behind the bushes, naked and alone, beaten and blood-soaked.

"The Mind of a Rapist," an article in the July 23, 1990, *Newsweek,* described "James," a forty-two-year-old Miami business manager with four children, who was aware only of a vague "frustration" in his life, and who liked to pick up women in pairs and rape one of them in front of the other. He explained, "Inside is a rage." Anger, "deep and dark," is a common thread among rapists, the authors pointed out. "Something has invariably gone wrong with their lives, often from the very beginning. A 1982 study of rapists in Oregon found that as many as 80 percent were abused children, and their victimization results in a kind of emotional death."

But when gangs set out in so-called wolf packs, this is a far more open declaration of fury. The victim does not stand a chance to escape. If the gang is murderous enough, as the Central Park attackers seemed to be, striking the jogger with a heavy pipe, injuring her brain, leaving her for dead, brutally disfiguring her face, we have to conclude, according to psychologist Nicholas Groth, director of Forensic Mental Health Associates, who has seen more than three thousand sex offenders in twenty-five years of practice, that "We look at rape as the sexual expression of aggression, rather than as the aggressive expression of sexuality."

Broadly speaking, he says, "Rapists fall into three motivational types, anger, power and sadism." Power rape, such as the Central Park attackers showed, is "a form of compensation committed usually by men who feel unsure of their competence." Or, as Richard Seely, director of Minnesota's Intensive Treatment Program for Sexual Aggressiveness, puts it, "It's the rapist's thinking that is dysfunctional, not his sexuality."

"Rage!" was the one-word headline of the front page of the *New York Post* on September 1, 1989. This accompanied photographs of an injured policeman and a description of protestors cuffed by the police: "23 cops hurt in clash with demonstrators protesting the 'brutal murder' of a black teen by several whites wielding baseball bats in Bensonhurst, Brooklyn." This murder showed the white man's unreal fear of blacks from the day they were imported from Africa. Many reasons are given for it, including the "jungle background of primitive men who have not learned to control anger," and thus the fear of being killed by anyone who possesses a dark skin.

Some psychologists refer to our culture as a "hate" culture, and cite the many murders of a wife or husband who is no longer wanted or who possesses money that the murderer stands to inherit. Sometimes hit men are sought to commit the deed. Or the spouse will figure out "subtle" ways to carry out the killing, such as placing a bomb in the victim's car or using poison.

Another kind of murder exists in households between husband and wife or parent and child. It is called "soul murder." This refers to the steady tearing down, both in words and deeds, of a person's emotional stamina until he feels unfit to live and gradually deteriorates.

Regardless of the context in which a killing takes place, the murderer is almost always despondent, depressed, and frustrated. Very frequently he feels friendless and misunderstood.

In any discussion of murder the question is always asked, "Is aggression an instinct, something we are born with and seek to gratify?" This has been debated for decades without apparent agreement among experts, regardless of their particular line of thought.

Freud, who started our look "inward," spoke constantly of hate and sadism but attributed them to frustration of the "erotic drive, as in the Oedipus complex," where hatred for the parent of the opposite sex was a natural feeling. In a letter to Dr. Wilhelm Fliess (May 13, 1897), he wrote that hostile wishes against parents, stemming from childhood, were "an integral part" of the depression that follows a loss.

In some people, Freud said, these hostile wishes come to light consciously in the form of obsessional ideas. In paranoia the delusions of persecution—the imagined murderous threats by unseen and unknown enemies—arise from the person's wish to kill someone to whom he is close, someone he feels threatens his life. Because the wish to kill is dangerous to his own survival, he projects it on others. Freud said there was "a fragment of fact" in the paranoiac's accusation that the mother or father of infancy either physically or psychologically threatened his life.

Freud also pointed out that feelings of abandonment always hold both grief and rage toward the one who deserts. He stated that the "roots of war" start in the nursery, implying it is the hatred between mother and child that plants the seeds of the child's later destructive tendencies.

In 1909 Freud wrote that "every act of hate issues from erotic tendencies," still tying hate to sex. In 1914 he introduced the concept of "narcissism," which included the urge of self-preservation: hate was summoned to ward off threats to life, either physical or psychological. Then he became dissatisfied with this concept and, in 1915, wrote that hate was distinct from the sexual drive and was "a primary part of the ego." This marked the start of his concept of a nonsexual part of the ego, in opposition to the sexual drive.

Freud pointed out that even the sexual instinct cannot be expressed without some measure of aggression and "therefore in the regular combination of the two instincts there is a partial sublimation of the destructive instinct." He added that "curiosity, the impulse to investigate," may be regarded as a complete sublimation of the aggressive or destructive impulse.

The hatred of a parent for a child and the effect on the child was mentioned by Freud in 1931 in "Female Sexuality." He described the early attachment of a daughter to her mother as closely connected to the cause of neurosis. He speculated that excessive dependence on the mother contained "the germ of later paranoia in women." He described this "germ" as "the surprising, yet regular, dread of being killed (?), devoured by the mother" (the question mark is Freud's). This dread of the mother, he said, may arise from an unconscious hostility on the mother's part, which the child senses.

The greatest hindrance to man's further development is his inability to deal in better fashion with his aggression and destructiveness, according to the late Dr. Ralph R. Greenson, author of *The Technique and Practice of Psychoanalysis,* who tried in vain to save the life of Marilyn Monroe, when she sought his help the last year of her life.

"I believe that for man to survive he must learn to curb, tame, channelize, and sublimate his aggressiveness and destructiveness," Greenson wrote. "To do this he must first face more honestly his greed, his envy, his hatred and fear of the stranger, and his hatred and fear of change. Only then can unconscious destructive guilt be changed to conscious guilt which can be controlled and useful. If we do this, man will have made a giant step forward, even if it is not to Point Omega."

As the late Maria W. Piers, author of *Infanticide,* wrote, "Not every brutalized and grossly neglected child grows up to be a Charles Manson. On the other hand, virtually every Charles Manson was once a neglected and abused child." ·

Thus we are born with two main drives, the aggressive and the sexual. By sexual, we mean not only adult sexual passion and intercourse but the wish for intimacy, closeness and attachment. A baby's wish to suck at the breast, to be held and to attach himself in a lasting relationship to his mother, is the formation of the sexual drive. As the child grows, these wishes become expressed in his desire for intimacy in all kinds of ties, including friendship as well as sexual relationships.

There is a vast difference between healthy, adaptive aggression, which we all need to get us through the day, and what has been called "murderous aggression." The former enables us to assert ourselves, work in comparative peace, solve conflicts fairly easily, and swing a golf club or a bat at a ball—not at another human being.

This aggression does not hold hostility but provides us with energy to be used in the service of coping, achieving, being thoughtful, and loving others. It is a nonhostile, nondestructive aggression, and it is instinctual. We use this "adaptive aggression" to attack a potential rapist or burglar or even to kill a potential murderer who threatens our life.

Although some, such as the anthropologist Konrad Lorenz, would disagree, it is our conviction and the conviction of most of those in the mental health professions that the rageful, hostile, murderous type of aggression is not something we are born with but a reaction to frustration, deprivation, threats, and blows to our self-esteem. It is formed in the early years of our life. To understand ourselves, we must be aware of our capacity for malevolence and the causes of such feelings.

The loving, mentally healthy man or woman with limited feelings of revenge, who uses aggression in a constructive way, may be more of an ideal than a reality. Most of us have had to endure many deprivations and frustrations that often do not appear reasonable or loving. They exist in our childhood and also in our adulthood. While no one enjoys hating, nor is anyone relaxed and happy when he wishes to kill, most of us sometimes experience feelings of hatred.

Groups of children and adults have been asked, "Is there anyone here who has had perfect parents?" Of thousands interviewed, not one said, "Yes, I had a perfect mother and father." Therefore, there is probably no human being alive fully exempt from destructive and murderous fantasies, although such feelings obviously occur in enormously varying degrees.

But the more a culture provides a child with two parents who love each other and who, the child feels, live and work together fairly peacefully to meet the emotional, physical, economic, and social needs of themselves and the child, the less destructive aggression will appear.

Perhaps because we live in a time when divorce is so popular and single parenthood so common, we may not fully face how rage, violence, and murder are more apt to occur in one-parent families. The child in such a family witnesses various forms of hatred and sometimes physical abuse between parents who soon separate. The child assumes that screaming, fighting, and abusing are a way of life. Furthermore, a parent who is divorced or a widower or widow has experienced much unhappiness as a rule and often cannot lovingly and spontaneously nurture the child. The irritability and tension within the parent becomes communicated to the child and the child, feeling unloved, sometimes also deserted, feels vengeance and spite. Most children from broken homes believe their "badness" created the schism between their parents and, feeling "bad," they often behave belligerently and provocatively.

There has probably been more confusion, as we have pointed out, about the term "aggression" than any other word in human discourse. Aggression as a response to a realistic threat is both healthy and adaptive. Violent rage and intense hatred, always a response to extreme threat and a strong feeling of deprivation, rarely serve anybody well—perpetrator or victim.

It is not unusual for someone to sit in a restaurant and wait endlessly for a waiter to take his order. The diner becomes irritated because he is ignored at a time he is hungry. The emotionally mature person, who feels realistically deprived of food when he is famished, may walk up to the waiter or the maître d' and say quietly but firmly, "I've been waiting to be served for over twenty minutes. Please arrange for me to be served as soon as possible. Thank you."

Each of us responds to frustration in his own unique way, much of it learned within the family. Many of us have been trained to cope with frustration by not saying a word. If, in a restaurant, we are kept waiting for food, we just walk out of the restaurant without complaining or explaining. While this may have an impact on our heartbeat and gastrointestinal system, we feel a certain degree of pleasure if we know this is what our parents would approve of, even though hunger strikes have their negative consequences. There are, however, usually nearby restaurants to serve us far more swiftly.

Some who give in to their rage might grab a waiter as he passes and roar, "Goddamn it, how long do I have to wait for my order to be taken?" This is the reaction of a narcissistic child who feels he has the right to immediate gratification the minute he yearns for something. Often this behavior incites others to act the same way because many of us remain in part narcissistic children and have to monitor this wish much of the time.

Eating in a restaurant may make many of us feel like a little child yearning to be fed immediately so we will not starve to death. The more we wish to be a child again, offered food instantly and adoringly, the more being kept waiting for twenty minutes seems like an insult—a severe deprivation, a blow to our ego.

If you feel like a child, you believe you deserve immediate attention. And if you do not receive it, you are then the victim of an acute rage that appears justified. The waiter or maître d' appears like a cruel, tyrannical mother, and you feel you have the right to scream, stamp your feet or even strike out if your slightest wish remains ungratified for long.

Under the influence of alcohol, some angry souls in restaurants or bars have struck a waiter or a bartender. When we are inebriated, we feel less controlled, more open to anger. We tend to reveal more of our buried feelings. Inattentive waitresses can appear like withholding mothers, and thus become the recipient of assault, usually verbal, for there is little support for men who strike women in public places.

The more we feel threatened in any way, the more we resort to primitive forms of aggression that include shouting, screaming, and striking or actual destruction of objects and people. The murderer feels the most threatened of all, otherwise he would not be driven to kill.

It is when we believe a threat to our very existence is imminent and danger great that we may act in an infantile way. The rage becomes more and more powerful and the potential for murder mounts. A young lawyer, married five years, felt consumed by anger one night because his wife, an actress, told him he had no "taste" in his choice of plays. She charged him with always choosing rowdy, erotic ones rather than those that would make him reflect about life. This was not the first time she had accused him of being "ignorant." After two stiff scotches before dinner, he found his fury escalating.

He felt like striking her for demeaning him. He walked over to where she sat in a chair and raised his hand. When he saw the look of fear on her face, he dropped his hand and said quietly, "I feel like killing you for being such a bitch, but I guess I have to remember that it takes all kinds to make a world."

He walked out of the apartment and out of her life; the couple soon divorced. He felt that her constant put-downs were both mental and sexual attacks. The fact that she could not accept his taste in plays made him feel like a "street peddler," and he decided he would not tolerate such attacks any longer. To this lawyer, his wife's criticism was experienced as annihilation. Thus he had to destroy his marriage, to make his wife suffer as he had suffered.

It is important to keep in mind that threats and dangers are perceived by each person in his own unique, idiosyncratic manner. What appears of little consequence to one person may be dangerous and threatening to another. To tell a man who prides himself on his athletic ability and virility that he is a "nerd" could be a disastrous remark. He may suddenly regress to the state of a furious child and kill the one who has criticized his abilities and sexuality. He feels as if he has suffered a dagger to his heart. Many a man not confident of his sexual potency has been known to become physically assaultive, even murderous, when a lover or wife attacks his masculinity.

Most people who are successful in their professions, particularly in politics, sports, and the entertainment industry, activate jealousy and resentment in the less successful. The more success we enjoy, especially if it brings great acclaim, the more we will be the recipient of derogatory remarks, even from family and supposedly dear friends.

Despite the enormous popularity of Presidents like Franklin D. Roosevelt and John F. Kennedy, the hatred toward these men was also intense. In the 1940s, Westbrook Pegler, a columnist for the *New York Journal-American,* devoted three columns a week for years damning President Roosevelt's acts. And although it is nearly thirty years since President Kennedy was murdered, books implying that he was dishonest, adulterous, and egocentric are still being written.

The secure politician, who is aware of a sense of purpose and self-identity, does not feel endangered. He is able to debate issues, disagree clearly and firmly with his angered opponents. That is, if he does not feel like a child and expect to be loved by everybody, for then he will feel in a constant rage. He may become physically assaultive, even murderous, or sink into deep depression.

In any discussion of how our murderous wishes evolve, it is important to keep in mind that most children and most adults try their best to deny and repress their violent thoughts because rage, hatred, and the idea of murder never feel bearable for long.

Furthermore, as we have indicated, the murderous impulse is most commonly felt toward those we need—need desperately at times—such as parents and siblings, and later, spouses, bosses, and colleagues. Many serious emotional illnesses are wishful expressions of murder turned against the self rather than against another person.

Let us consider some examples from everyday life. Depression, whether moderate or severe, results from a feeling of the loss of love. It contains a buried anger that cannot be discharged because it has been relegated to the part of the mind that is unconscious. The child or adult who is insulted (in fantasy or reality) may feel rejected (in fantasy or reality) by someone he believes he needs desperately. He cannot discharge or even acknowledge to himself his inevitable anger. Instead, he feels depressed and sorry for himself.

A woman of fifty, a writer of self-help books, was aghast one evening when her best friend of twenty-two years, a female advertising executive, turned on her after downing three glasses of wine and said contemptuously, "Your latest book is a downer. You really can't write. I'm a better writer than you."

The woman felt a surge of fury at her supposed friend. She wanted to throw her out of the apartment, scream at her, never see her again, kill her off this way. But because of what she had learned about herself during three years of therapy, she understood her own jealousy of those who were successful and held back her temper.

Instead, she looked grimly at her friend, changed the subject, and asked, "Shall we go to dinner?" She realized that her friend had often emotionally supported her over the years and that it was her jealousy, released by the wine, which had driven her to speak of her angry, envious feelings. The writer accepted her friend's outburst even though for the moment it made her feel demeaned and thus furious.

As they left the apartment, the advertising executive turned and said, as though in apology, "You know I really love you."

The writer smiled and answered, "I love you, too," adding to herself, "at least most of the time."

As we understand the rage and hatred within ourselves and accept it as part of being human, we understand the rage and hatred in others. We do not condemn or forsake them but enjoy them for the part that is friendly, loving, warm.

Many of us yearn for a love that is so unrealistic we will go to extremes to try to get it from an unloving parent, lover, or spouse. Psychologists call this "masochism." The masochistic person in effect begs, "Hit me, beat me, demean me, as long as you don't leave me."

Underneath his suffering, the masochist holds back extreme fury but is not aware of his wish to avenge himself. He believes that if he felt his rage, he would kill—that "the wish is the same as the deed." Instead, he vicariously enjoys the sadism of his parent, lover, or spouse as the other person acts out his own forbidden wish. It is as though the masochist is screaming, "See how I suffer, well, this is how I wanted you to suffer but did not dare attack you."

The masochist covers his sadism from himself and others. He is the last to acknowledge he feels sadistic at times. Masochism is perhaps best understood in the case of wives who continue to take severe physical and psychological abuse from the husbands they believe they need in order to survive. Like children, they feel if they are left alone they will wither away. They have no resources to go it alone—something only an adult can do in both an emotional and physical sense.

Although there are several points of view about the cause of schizophrenia, including perspectives that suggest a genetic predisposition, it is our conviction that the schizophrenic embodies an extreme form of turning hostile aggression on the self. Such a deeply troubled person is terrified of his strong, murderous wishes. He creates his own private world of delusions and hallucinations, rather than face the fact that he would like to kill his parents, siblings, and all those he believes have hurt him over the years. Sometimes schizophrenics act out their murderous feelings, let loose their long-concealed hate.

The person who sits alone in a mental hospital, unable to communicate with others, talking to himself, fantasying he is someone else, usually a god or a copilot of God, is filled with hatred and unable to face his feelings. We also see this in many of the homeless who now roam our streets, asking piteously to be taken care of, given a small pittance for a meal. They are not much different from the pained child they once were—the child in all of us to some degree.

To understand why we feel murderous or become murderous, we have to understand the threats and angers common to all of us. The most serious threat is the real or imagined loss of a person we need, whose love we considered essential to our survival. This starts with the mother of childhood, without whose care we die. Even among animals, when a mother cow is separated from her calf, she becomes murderous and destructive until she gets him back. She probably possesses the knowledge that he cannot survive alone.

Most murders that take place among lovers and spouses are caused when one of them threatens or demands the end of the relationship. Because none of us ever quite gives up the child who remains, we are all potential killers when we are or feel we may be abandoned by someone we hold crucial to our life. Joseph Kallinger's murderous existence was a direct response to the actual abandonment he experienced early in life from his real mother, then the emotional abandonment by his unbelievably cruel foster parents. The more we feel our early loved ones are available to give love, the less possibility there is we will feel hate or act murderously.

Closely related to the threat of abandonment is the threat that love will be taken away, even though the parent, lover, or friend remains present. If a mother says to a child, "I don't love you any more," when he misbehaves, watch the child's response. He will either kick someone or some toy, scream as if the house were on fire, or become depressed and withdrawn.

The more acutely we feel the love of a particular person is essential, the more desperate we become when we believe love is not forthcoming, that we are being scorned. As William Congreve wrote in 1697 in his play *The Mourning Bride:* "Heaven has no rage like love to hatred turned, nor hell a fury like a woman scorned." We may expand the analogy: ". . . like anyone scorned by someone whose love is vital." That includes all of us, man or woman, child or adult, black or white or yellow, successful or unsuccessful.

We can more readily understand some of the murders in the last few decades if we keep in mind that the murderer felt a crucial love had been ripped away from him. In most cases he was cruelly treated as a child, whipped by a murderous parent or ignored almost completely and felt abandoned. Some of our Presidential assassins may be viewed as would-be lovers whose childhood frustrations finally exploded.

Sirhan Sirhan killed Robert Kennedy because in large part he felt like a jilted lover, as some of his written imaginary conversations with Kennedy showed. He rationalized his disappointment by saying he was politically frustrated but he felt psychologically jilted. His rage was part of his hatred for a father who punished him severely when he disobeyed as a child. We might also say that Sirhan's yearning for Kennedy was like that of a child's desire for the one in power, the man "at the top" like his father, even though the latter once tried to kill his son by burning his feet.

Arthur Bremer, who crippled Governor George Wallace, fantasized a private love affair between himself and the Governor for several years. Like Sirhan, he kept clippings, speeches, and pictures of the Governor all over his room, another sign of the jilted lover. We can assume there was violence in Bremer's early life that caused him to try to murder Governor Wallace.

While each assassin has his own idiosyncratic past and unique lifestyle, several generalizations are possible. All the assassins felt deeply rejected and frustrated about the inconsistency or absence of tender loving care in their early life. Researchers on child development have found that when a child does not receive sufficient gratification in the form of physical holding and hugging, as well as psychological holding and hugging, his first response is hostile protest.

We can see hostile protest even in the young infant whose mother or mother substitute is away too long—frequently the case with the future assassin. Often, the assassin has never seen his parents act lovingly toward each other. Rather, he has witnessed feuding and fighting, as one of the parents, usually the father, takes off, often permanently.

Yet all of us to some degree are would-be killers, for none of us can ever be loved all the time by those whose love we crave consistently. The more threatened we are by the absence of love in childhood, which means the presence of intense hatred, the more murderous we become.

In recent years we have seen an obsession on the part of some murderers with killing famous people. Many of these fervent admirers will follow actors, actresses, singers, all over the country. When they realize their love will not be reciprocated, they wish to kill the object of their desperate passion.

An example of one such admirer who turned into a crazed attacker is the killer of John Lennon. Mark David Chapman worshiped the rock singer and wrote him numerous letters. There was no response and he finally shot Lennon as he stood outside his home at Central Park West and Seventy-second Street in Manhattan.

One of the ways to activate murderous wishes in someone is to stop talking to them. When we are not acknowledged, we feel devalued and hated, as if the person who will not speak is trying to get rid of us; we believe he is in effect saying we do not exist. Feeling acutely rejected, if not psychologically murderous, we seek revenge. Many a temper tantrum in a child and an adult, even to the point of violence and murder, is a response to being disregarded. When someone talks to us we feel of some importance to them even if their words are angry ones. But silence is often experienced as annihilation and the one who feels annihilated wishes in turn to annihilate.

A second way to induce murderous feelings within someone is by severe threats to the body. Any physical attempt to injure or hurt us produces the murderous wish, for the potential loss of an organ or a limb constitutes a deadly threat. Unless we are masochistic, most of us hate going to the dentist for the removal of a tooth. The dentist, we imagine, lies ready to hurt or injure us and the more vulnerable we feel, the more we hate him. Children, even adults, have been known to bite the dentist's finger or kick him in the groin.

Any threat to the body induces an immediate murderous response. Whether a child is about to undergo a tonsillectomy, or an adult a gall bladder operation, neither can endure this threat without feeling hatred and the wish to murder the doctor.

If the usually gentle dentist, who realistically exists to help us keep our teeth, becomes the object of violence, how do we feel toward someone who really is out to harm us? Such as a rapist, a burglar, or a drug addict on the street ready to kill us if we do not hand over our money?

More common, however, is the murderous reaction turned against the self. The person undergoing a mastectomy or amputation feels more depressed than outwardly angry as he hastily assigns his wish to kill to the unconscious, believing in this way it will leave him. Instead, unless he becomes consciously aware of it, it will build up over the frustrating years.

It is constructive to feel intense anger when confronted with a loss in the body. If more physicians and hospitals recognized this, many would be spared depression, agitation, and suffering. An understanding doctor who has to perform surgery, or a sympathetic dentist who takes out a tooth, would be kind and helpful if he could say, "I know this makes you very angry and upset. I don't blame you. I'd feel the same."

Another way to induce murderous feelings is by threats to the image of the self. All of us, man or woman, child or adult, want others to experience us in a flattering manner. Some aspire to be superathletes. Others wish to be brilliant intellectuals. Still others want to be told consistently they are handsome or beautiful.

We all desire to have certain traits of character acknowledged and appreciated. Some wish to be considered kind, others resourceful. If someone accuses us of being unkind, or tells us we are cruel or uncooperative, rage can be our response.

Call a man who aspires to be macho effeminate and he will want to kill. Tell a woman whose physical attractiveness is essential to her identity that she is unattractive and she will want to kill. Tell a professor that he is stupid or an athlete that he is a lousy player and he will "see red" for murder.

A threat to our status brings rage. Whether we admit it or not, we all wish to feel superior to somebody. Tell an Army lieutenant he is going to be demoted and he will feel like killing. Tell an administrator or an executive he is going to be relegated to a mere rank-and-file member and he will wish to kill.

Violence often occurs when someone suddenly demoted feels that the act was unwarranted—the way most of us would feel. The baseball player asked to warm the bench invariably believes he should be on the field. Feeling unwanted, he will frequently fly into a rage.

In our society's growing attempt to achieve equality between the sexes and between races and religions, many a man is furious when a woman is made his superior, as he feels this is unwarranted. Many whites experience the same reaction when blacks become their superiors, or other members of a minority are given high status.

Threats to status, like all threats, will be experienced by different individuals in their own ways. If in the person's mind a particular title or status is crucial to his existence, the danger of that loss appears ominous and the potential for rage runs deep.

Whenever the murderous wish is aroused, it is always the result of a feeling of deprivation or injustice. It may be real, such as the loss of income. Or it may be fantasied, such as the loss of love, or when blacks or other members of minority groups, including gay men and women, are unfairly deprived of their civil and economic rights.

The murderous wish becomes stirred up when we think we are treated unfairly and arbitrarily, usually by a person in power. A private in the Army will feel far more murderous toward an insulting sergeant who calls him lazy than toward another private who makes the same charge. The private cannot say "Go to hell!" to the sergeant, but he can say this to his buddy without fear of revenge and punishment.

Even teasing can make us feel murderous. If we believe we are entitled to something and it is taken away, this infuriates us. Promise a child ice cream but renege on the promise and you see a temper tantrum explode. Promise any man or woman enhanced status or opportunity, then take the promise away and you will often see murderous rage.

The murderous wish always implies revenge. "An eye for an eye, a tooth for a tooth," and a murderous wish for what appears as a murderous attack.

It is important to keep in mind what we will continue to stress: We are all potential murderers—the difference between a Hinckley who really tries to kill the President of the United States and a depressed, jealous lover who sits in his room and just fantasies killing his rival, is a matter of degree.

None of us can possess everything, or be everything we wish. All of us have to cope with mild, moderate, or severe frustrations and deprivations. The more these frustrations and deprivations threaten us, the more vulnerable we feel and the greater the wish to attack.

Not only what the perpetrator or the victim thinks crucial in the misunderstanding of a violent act, but what others think in the present or what they thought in the past about the act, is often vital to its understanding. Joan of Arc was considered a heroine because she obeyed an inner voice that ordered her to go and kill the enemy. Her actions were applauded by many who surrounded her. Abraham heard the voice of God telling him to sacrifice his son, Isaac, so that he felt a certain sanctioning of his murderous act. Today Joan of Arc would be considered paranoid for hearing voices and Abraham would be considered a child abuser.

All murderers, whether verbal tongue-lashers or sadistic killers, have real or imagined audiences watching and in communication with them. Sometimes these audiences are supporters, sometimes enemies. A murderer is always an exhibitionist—he needs to know, or he imagines, someone is watching his act of cuelty. Joseph Kallinger held numerous dialogues with God. Here he was similar to Abraham and others in the Bible who communicated with God.

Many of us watch movies and plays that depict murder. Why are we torn in half as we watch? Part of us insists the murderer be caught for his perfidious act. But another, very strong part exults in the act of murder as we identify with the killer. He acts out the revenge within our hearts. For a moment, we can be honest with ourselves as we feel somewhat freer. We have temporarily lifted rage from the unconscious part of our mind where it simmers away year after year.

It is important to recognize how many movies and plays depict violence and murder. This tells much about our society—that there are murderous wishes in all our hearts and we need to vicariously discharge them. A peaceful, cooperative society that engenders more love than hatred would probably have limited use for murder mysteries, violence in all forms, and criminal activity. The media's preoccupation with murder reflects a society that endorses murder psychologically, if not legally.

PART 2

The Seeds of Murder

3

The Wish to Murder in Childhood

"Childhood has become far more precarious and less safe for millions of America's children," a 1989 Congressional study concluded.

March 6, 1989, was a snowy day, and the Polk Township Elementary School in Kresgeville, a rural village twenty-five miles south of Stroudsburg in the Pocono region of Pennsylvania, was closed down.

Cameron Robert Kocher, nine years and ten months old, walked next door when his parents, Keith, a laborer, and Patricia, a sewing machine operator in a dress factory, went to work. They had decided he should spend the day with their neighbors, the Rattis, who had a seven-year-old daughter, Jessica, a first-grader at the school. Another family, the Carrs, also deposited their daughter, Shannon, thirteen, at the Rattis' house.

The three children played the new Nintendo game Jessica had just received. She boasted she could play it better than Cameron, who loved the game but did not own a set.

At one point late in the morning, after eating, the three children were forced to stop the game as punishment because they had left dirty cups and bowls lying around. They dressed warmly and went outside to play, for the snow had temporarily ceased. Cameron complained he thought it unfair that he be punished because he had not contributed to any of the mess.

He left the two girls and tramped through the snow to return home. According to later testimony in court, he went to his parents' second-floor bedroom and reached inside the base of a lamp to get the key to his father's gun cabinet, having often seen his father do this. He opened the cabinet and, from the ten rifles in it used to hunt deer, he selected a high-powered hunting rifle, a .35-caliber Marlin with a sling and scope. He unlocked an ammunition drawer, found the proper bullets, loaded the rifle, climbed on the bed, opened the window, and removed the screen.

It was one o'clock. About three hundred feet from him in the yard of the Ratti home he saw Jessica and Shannon riding a snowmobile, moving slowly at walking speed. He aimed the gun at Jessica. As Shannon later testified, she felt Jessica suddenly fall against her. She said, "I figured something must be wrong with her. I looked at her and her eyes were rolled up back into her head."

Cameron removed the spent cartridge and hid it in the box of bullets. He replaced the rifle and relocked the cabinet. Shannon's father, summoned to their house, called Cameron on the telephone, asking him to return to the Rattis' because "a sniper was loose" and he did not want Cameron to be hurt too.

Several persons later testified that when Cameron entered the Ratti house, he walked past the living room where Jessica lay dying and turned the video game back on. He told Shannon, "If you don't think about it, you won't be sad."

When the state police arrived, they noticed a crescent-shaped cut on Cameron's forehead that they later said looked as though it could have been caused by the scope of a recoiling rifle. They went next door to his house, found blood in the upstairs bedroom and on the rifle. Two days later they arrested him.

When examined by a psychiatrist, Cameron said he had been inside his house looking out a window through the rifle scope, playing hunter, but all he could see were trees and snow. He said he "touched something" and the gun went off. Evidently he had been imitating his father shooting at a deer, only Cameron's deer was Jessica, who had boasted she was a better Nintendo player than he was.

Mark P. Pazuhanich, the first assistant district attorney in Monroe County, viewed the deliberate steps Cameron took before firing the rifle as evidence that he intended to shoot Jessica. Pazuhanich pointed out that Cameron had left the Ratti house in a very angry state, that he was furious about being kept from playing the video game and in addition deeply resented being punished for dirtying the dishes, something he did not do.

Why does a boy of nine commit murder? Is it enough to say he was jealous of Jessica for possessing a toy he did not own? Was he furious at her for taunting him that she was "better" then he was at the game? Did her mother's punishment of him, though he believed he was innocent, add to his fury?

Was it the fact that being an only child made it too difficult for him to share anything with symbolic siblings? Was he a highly narcissistic, angry boy who wanted what he wanted when he wanted it? Did he perhaps hate girls? How much did his parents, particularly his father, subtly encourage him to murder by leaving guns in the house? Was his mother a cold, hostile woman who never truly gave him love? What took place in the nine years of Cameron's life that brought out a violence that led to murder? Some of these questions, perhaps all of them, may be pertinent in trying to fathom Cameron's devastating destruction of a seven-year-old girl.

When does the life of a murderer begin?

The life of a murderer—the origin of his wrath—starts when all life begins, at conception. We now have proof that the nine months in the womb affect a child deeply. The unborn child is not merely a passive embryo but also an active, feeling human organism. Careful studies of the reactions of a fetus in the womb show that as early as twenty-five weeks a fetus will jump in time to a drumbeat, will respond to the sounds around him, including music, and will suck or grimace when he tastes sweet or sour liquids.

From the sixth month on, the unborn baby is able to learn. In a classic study, medical investigators taught sixteen unborn babies to respond to a specific cue by kicking. We know that from the seventh month on, the unborn child hears, sees, tastes, and feels on a primitive level. He is starting to shape his personality from "messages" both parents send.

The father, if he understands and loves his wife, influences her feelings and, through her, the well-being of the fetus. But if the father is angry, brutal, uncaring toward his wife, this will make her feel depressed and unwanted, and she will feel the same way toward the fetus, possibly blaming it for her husband's wrath.

How the unborn child feels about his environment in the womb is closely related to how the prospective mother experiences her own life. How she experiences the prospect of the child's birth is also crucial to his development. We know that when the prospective mother feels emotionally gratified in her marriage, pleased with her day-to-day existence, this will have an effect on how secure the fetus feels. Also, the degree to which she wants to have a baby (perhaps most if not all women are ambivalent to some degree) will affect the fetus.

If a prospective mother is subjected to deep frustration, her body reacts and the fetus feels this. Therefore, he does not develop in a healthy environment. During the first third of pregnancy, studies show that if the prospective mother undergoes great stress, the fetus may develop, among other dysfunctions, a cleft palate. And babies born of mothers who have experienced emotional, economic, or physical stress are often premature.

We know that babies born to mothers using crack or

other drugs have serious difficulties relating to their world, making friends, playing like normal children, and feeling love for their mothers or primary caretakers. We also know that children of addicted mothers may be unable to develop into adults who can relate easily to others.

The importance of prenatal life is perhaps illustrated best by the Chinese. They assign the day of conception as the birthday. Consequently, they consider the child already nine months old at birth.

If we think of a child at birth as nine months old, then how much emotional and physical nourishment he receives during those nine months is an important factor in determining how many seeds of murder lie in the womb. If his mother is under abnormal stress with physical or emotional problems, the unborn child will have a higher potential for murder.

Many studies show the definite correlation between birth trauma and later psychological problems. Some scientists have even gone so far as to aver that the minutes and hours following birth may be the most important in a child's life. The atmosphere in hospitals counts—whether the doctor is tired or welcoming, the nurse's attitude, the attendant's concern. The feelings of the prospective father—how much he wants a baby, whether he wishes a boy or girl, whether the baby is his first or third—are also crucial factors in forming the baby's personality.

Often a father will love and identify most with the baby who arrives in the same order the father did as a child. This is true of the mother too. Some parents with low self-esteem may feel negatively toward the child who is in the same birth order as they were. This can determine how the child is greeted—with love or hate or indifference—and will affect how the child greets the world, whether with love and hope or with hatred and depression.

A Cesarean delivery no doubt affects the mother's attitude toward the child. If the birth process or the pregnancy is unpleasant for the mother, she is bound to feel certain resentments toward the baby. And the baby in turn will feel unwelcome.

Many mothers who have had Cesareans or other difficulties during the carrying of the baby may harbor hostile feelings toward the youngster. Some men and women who have seen psychotherapists and admitted they have come close to murder at times, or who actually did murder someone and served a term in prison, said that their mothers informed then, "You almost killed me when you were born." If we are told by the one who conceived us that we are a born killer, we are sure to believe it. It is the opinion of the most powerful authority in our lives.

Perhaps more important than prenatal life and the birth process is what transpires during the first few weeks of life and during the first year. We know the capacity for mature emotional relationships in adult life is a direct outgrowth of parental care. More specifically, the kind of mothering an infant receives will strongly affect his entire life.

Chances are high that the child, then the adult, will become more loving and less hateful if he is adequately fed and made comfortable during the first few months of life. The feeling of being wanted, loved, and played with is an extremely important part of the infant's emotional diet. The intake of nourishment and the intake of good will should proceed simultaneously.

If an infant has been deprived of warm fondling and becomes the recipient of careless, haphazard feeding so that he has to cry a long time before his food arrives, inevitably he becomes an angry, bitter child who cannot be pleased. As an adult he will frequently make "biting" remarks and "chew out" others. Adults cannot feel tender and close to anyone if they have not received tender, loving care during the first year of life. This is a basic psychological truth.

Psychologists have shown that the paranoid personality, one who is constantly suspicious of other people, imagines that hatred exists wherever he goes. He himself is filled with hatred and usually has been brought up in a "poor" environment. He becomes unresponsive, rarely understanding himself or anyone else.

A "poor" environment refers not only to economic poverty but to the more crucial emotional poverty, which leads to an inability to relate to others in a warm, intimate, understanding fashion. The seeds of paranoia can be planted in wealthy homes if a child is neglected, unloved, and treated indifferently or with anger and hatred. Gloria Vanderbilt's difficult emotional childhood was tragic, although she was very wealthy. The suicide of one of her sons shows that the sadness and emotional deprivation of "the poor little rich girl" somehow reached his psyche in ways that made him feel so depressed he did not want to live.

Readers of the description of the latest murder in our daily newspapers usually show surprise when the murderer comes from a middle- or upper-class family and has had all of life's comforts. The killer is less a mystery, however, if we consider the fact that despite the luxury in food, clothing, home, education, he lacks that part of the daily emotional diet that includes being wanted and loved as a small child.

There is also the fact that many parents treat a baby and growing child as their possession, not wanting to let him feel free and be someone in his own right. Feeling controlled or dominated, he may hate, perhaps even wish to kill to escape from these emotional tentacles. While the controlled and dominated child reacts with revenge, his murderous potential is less than that of a child who has been rejected or abused.

We stress throughout this book that how parents feel toward one another and toward the child determines in many ways how that youngster will develop in an emotional sense. We will explain in greater detail in Chapter 5 how parents relive their own childhoods through their children, but we wish to emphasize here that how parents feel toward their growing children will in many ways be a mirror of how they themselves were greeted at birth and responded to during childhood by their parents.

A mother who enjoys breast-feeding her infant was in all likelihood the recipient of warm breast-feeding when she was a child. The father who can take part in the nurturing of the infant, diapering him, putting him to sleep, holding him tenderly, probably had an attentive mother and father who helped him to a fairly contented, fulfilling life. But if mothers or fathers were abruptly weaned, prematurely toilet-trained, treated cruelly or ignored, the resentments and hatreds harbored from childhood will inevitably influence their own childrearing.

Specialists who work with children and parents have noted over and over that even when parents are extremely conscientious and vow, "I will never treat my child the way I was treated," frequently they still use their own parents as role models. Without consciously meaning to do so, they tend to repeat the same errors with their children that their own parents committed with them.

How a parent's sexual curiosity was responded to during his childhood will also influence how the parent answers questions about sex and how the parent helps the child cope with his loving and passionate feelings. For example, if a parent as a child was told overtly or covertly to inhibit his sexual curiosity, he may do the same with his child or, in revenge at his parents, be too active and too permissive. Similarly, if a parent as a child felt overstimulated, he may behave the same way, or if he felt he was the victim of abuse he may avoid helping his child become a sexual person.

It is not sufficiently appreciated that every parent, in one way or another, relives his own childhood while going through the various stages all parents must experience. A sensitive parent, an understanding parent, a loving parent, from time to time reviews his own childhood, particularly his relationship with his mother and father, to see if he is repeating his parents' mistakes or overreacting to them with his own children.

Parents who spank their children are convinced that this is necessary in order for them to grow into responsible young adults who behave themselves, but "the fact is, however, that punishments both mild and strong don't work," says Verne Faust, psychologist and former Dean of the School of Education, United States International University. "Worse, punishments are a disaster. The cost in human misery is horrendously exorbitant."

In his book *Five Ways of Parenting: One That Works,* Faust notes that a "do-nothing approach, however, carries with it its own destructiveness. Left without the predictability of firm boundaries that limit and guide undeveloped egos, youngsters' behavior is often destructive." Any anger expressed toward youngsters "leaves them unsure about themselves" and "self-esteem drops," he warns.

He concludes that parents, teachers and society "rely heavily, almost fully, on shame if the child does not measure up and the potential shame that always exists even when the child is successful. This shame inevitably, automatically, trips the rage center. The result: the guilt and anxiety created by resentment and rage felt toward others, especially loved ones and the anxiety of 'What will happen to me if I express this rage?' " This can become so painful, he points out, that "it is sent underground where inevitably it will have its day in neurotic defenses, attention deficits and other crippling behavior. And if these do not work, the impulses turn against organs of the body."

"One sees what the child will be the first year of his life," says Alma Halbert Bond, author of *Who Killed Virginia Woolf?* The child in the womb can be either active or passive. She points out, "I carried twins. One kicked all the time and the other I hardly knew was there. That's how it was all through childhood. The one who was hyperactive, the boy, is now a highly successful owner of his advertising agency. The other is a happily married woman with two children, not ambitious in any way. Freud said, 'Anatomy is destiny.' Physiology is destiny."

The well-known child therapist Erik Erikson described

the first year of life as "the trust/mistrust period." He meant that if a baby receives consistent, tender, loving care, he develops self-confidence and faith in those to whom he is close and to the world around him.

As pointed out earlier, because they are children unnurtured from birth, murderers do not trust the world. "The murderer has carried a keg of repressed rage all his life," as Bond, a psychoanalyst, put it.

Murderers are paranoid, distrustful, angry at everyone. When we cannot trust another person, we turn for gratification to inhuman "objects"—alcohol, drugs, or other means of pleasure that do not involve human beings. Under the influence of alcohol or other mood-altering substances, normal controls and inhibitions diminish and the wish to murder may become a reality, no longer fantasy. We know for certain that murder and other forms of violence may take place when someone loses his reason, so to speak, and the inner rage bursts forth.

Many murderers were unhappy, frustrated, furious babies who were later driven as adults to tell the world, "I can't get tender, loving care from anyone. I don't trust a soul, so I'll consume alcohol and feel warm inside." Such a person enjoys the warmth alcohol brings as it soothes him initially. But too much alcohol, as we know, stirs the underlying anger. Some wives have been killed when an alcoholic husband turns on them. *The Burning Bed,* a TV movie written by Robert Greenwald, reversed this, showing how a beaten, beleagured wife finally turned on her husband, set the house on fire, and escaped with her children.

Many an alcoholic feels furious because he has to rely on a shot of liquor rather than an embrace or kiss from someone who loves him. He is not aware he is unable to face his own emotional distress, which started in childhood, and drives him to select someone who is equally emotionally distressed.

It is more than a coincidence that after the furious baby within the adult relies for the feeling of warmth on a "shot" of scotch or gin or rye, he may then "shoot" a gun. It is not by accident that those who imbibe alcohol use the term "a shot" of scotch while drug addicts speak of "shooting up." These terms may be chosen unconsciously but they reveal the inner wish to kill the self or others.

To appreciate the murderous wishes in ourselves and understand the motives of murderers, we have to keep in mind that the wish to kill occurs when we feel very unloved, cannot love ourselves, and thus are unable to love anyone else. The less we love ourselves, the weaker and the more powerless we feel. We desperately seek moments that will make us feel we are the one in power, even if only for a short time and even if it may entail taking the life of someone else. We identify somehow with the powerful, murderous parent who has hurt us deeply as we now take control in forbidden fashion.

This is seen dramatically in the life of Willie James Bosket, Jr., as told by Sylvia Honig, interviewed for this book by Lucy Freeman. Honig, a social worker, lives in Nassau, New York, just east of Albany. Formerly she worked with the New York State Division for Youth, and first met Willie when he was twelve years old.

"Willie Bosket blames the prison system for turning him into the monster he is, a convicted murderer who threatens to maim and kill prison guards whenever he gets the chance," she said. In a July 24, 1988, letter to Joseph Demski, then deputy superintendent of security at the maxi-maxi Shawangunk State Prison, where Willie stabbed a guard in front of one hundred persons in the visiting room one Saturday afternoon, he offered himself as a guinea pig to psychiatrists and corrections authorities to find out "What makes Willie Bosket tick?"

"The offer was ignored," Honig reported. "The New York State prison authorities despise Willie and make no attempt to treat him as mentally ill. They regard him as a menace without redeeming virtues, their most dangerous prisoner, their most costly security problem, and a perfect rationale for the death penalty. He is a prison warden's nightmare."

She added, "Their sentiments are reciprocated. In an eight-page handwritten statement attached to the letter Willie wrote Demski, he expressed rage toward 'the system,' which he refers to as his 'surrogate mother,' because, he maintains, he has been reared by the State Division for Youth since the age of ten and has spent most of the last eighteen years of his twenty-seven years locked up." In this intensely angry statement, Willie describes the stabbing at Shawangunk in this unforgettable manner:

On April 16, 1988 at approximately 12:42 pm in the visiting room of the Shawangunk State Prison, prison guard Earl Porter felt a vicious hate-filled thrust as an eleven-inch stiletto blade was plunged into his chest to the hilt, just a fraction of an inch from penetrating his heart. The heart had definitely been the target. And as the stiletto blade invaded the chest cavity of prison guard Earl Porter, in search of his most vital organ, Bosket's most vital organ was singing a song of hateful joy.

To this day the only regret Bosket have [sic] is not having killed prison guard Earl Porter and spitting on his corpse—not because he was Earl Porter, but because he was "system." Hate knows no distinction when it comes to the monster lashing out, and I say this for all those who raised the fact that Bosket never knew or had any dealings with prison guard Earl Porter.

Honig said that "Willie's blood-curdling comments and vicious behavior earned him nationwide media attention, in which he revels, nicknames that have been splashed across newspapers, magazines and tabloids, including the *National Enquirer, Time, Newsday,* the *New York Post,* and *Daily News.* Reporters dubbed him 'Baby-Face Bosket, the Thrill Killer,' the 'Baby-Faced Butcher,' and the 'Self-

Styled Monster.' Willie seems proudest of the epithet 'New York's Most Dangerous Prisoner,' as he has been described by the media since the stabbing at Shawangunk."

"As the person who, besides his family members, knows him longer and better than anyone else," Honig says,

> I have been called and questioned dozens of times by reporters in quest of information about this notorious young killer. My sixteen-year friendship with Willie, which ended in December, 1989, when he banished me from his cell at Woodbourne State Prison (for disagreeing with him and not being "obedient") furnished me with reams of factual information on him, much of which he sent me in preparation for a book he asked me to write about his life. But the reporters were less interested in the facts than in my opinion about Willie's mental state. Indeed, since the brutal, near-fatal stabbing of Earl Porter, media people have asked me repeatedly whether Willie is a cold-blooded killer or a lunatic whose crimes stem from mental disease.
>
> I've told them that I think Willie is a paranoid schizophrenic who believes he must attack and kill others before they get him first. Superficially, he behaves in a normal manner when he wants to. He's particularly charming and rational whenever he receives visitors. But, like all severely disturbed people, his mood swings are sudden and violent, often provoked by something trivial, at times without rhyme or reason.
>
> At Brookwood Center, the state training school where I met Willie, he already showed severe emotional problems at age fourteen. Once he became violent when told by a staff member to stop smoking in the hall, another time for being refused permission to do a second sand art project in class, once when teased by other boys in his unit, often for just being denied extra privileges he demanded.

In March, 1978, fifteen-year-old Willie gunned down three men in the subway on three separate nights. According to his cousin, Herman Spates, who accompanied him during the killings, Willie selected his victims at random, demanded their money, and then gunned them down anyway after they had complied. Two of the men died. Willie's cousin told the court that Willie said he was killing for the fun of it and for the experience.

During his twelve years in maximum security state prisons, Willie has lived almost exclusively in "the box," the special housing units for dangerous prisoners, who are locked up twenty-three hours a day and always under close surveillance. As Willie is highly intelligent, it is clear that he lives in the box because he wants to. He tries to convince people that he's in the box because his jailors are so inhumane and so frightened of him that he's never given a chance to get into the prison population, but there is no credibility to that theory. Willie wants to be in the box for at least three good reasons: mainly, he distrusts everyone and fears he'll be killed unless he's securely isolated; two, he glories in his reputation as being so dangerous he needs ultrastrong security to be safely confined; and three, he has an insatiable lust for power and control. Being in the box means he gets constant close attention, his food and medicine are brought to him, Legal Aid attorneys work continuously for more humane conditions for him, and special rules apply to him, differentiating him from the thousands of other prisoners who are faceless numbers, doomed to live out their sentences in deprivation and anonymity without the comfort of making headlines, disrupting the system, and spitting on their enemies, both literally and figuratively, as Willie does all the time.

Drunk with dreams and aspirations of power and glory, Willie has entered into collaborative agreements with three people to write a book about his life. I was his first collaborator. Later he invited Matthew Worth, a reporter from a daily paper in Utica who covered one of Willie's infamous trials, and finally Fox Butterfield, the *New York Times* reporter.

Honig described him as "a bundle of contradictions as he was tagged by one New York City tabloid reporter. Willie constantly develops his closest relationships with white people while decrying white racism," she said.

Eventually, all these relationships are ruptured by his insatiable demands for attention, loyalty, respect, and service to help him beat the system and achieve the freedom that he obviously fears and avoids by assaulting guards and threatening to kill prison staff.

Many baffling questions about Willie Bosket persist. However, it has to be obvious to anyone who knows basic human behavior that Willie is far too angry and uncontrollable to be normal or sane or simply evil. His behavior screams out mental illness. The most obvious symptom is the unmitigated murderous rage that has enslaved him all his life. That rage, so long sustained, is not normal. It is fueled by schizophrenic terror, a recoil from the world, an inability to establish basic trust toward anyone, his progressive retreat into his own world where he makes the rules or believes he does, where he calls the shots and holds the power of life and death.

Any normal person would have become a screaming lunatic living under the totally constrained, isolated conditions that Willie has endured these past two years since the stabbing. He has his own private prison, a three-cell unit on the top floor of Woodbourne State Prison, monitored twenty-four hours a day on closed circuit TV, chained hand and foot when visitors see him or when he goes anywhere outside his cell, shut off from the world by a plexiglass wall completely surrounding the cell, with only tiny holes to shout through.

He cannot receive packages, make physical contact with family or friends, can never make or receive phone calls. He cannot watch television or operate a radio, though a guard can turn on an AM radio for him. Even during his one lonely hour in the prison yard for fresh air and exercise, he remains cuffed and shackled. Guards are not permitted to converse with him; they may only speak when it's necessary. There is silence and emptiness in his special lonely domain. Yet Willie remains rational on the surface, working regularly on his appeals and lawsuits against the state, conferring with his Legal Aid attorneys, laughing and joking with his visitors—except those like me who have displeased him and have been banished.

"Once it becomes indisputable that Willie is mentally deranged, the question of 'Why?' arises," Honig said, adding:

I can only speculate, but I think I know Willie better than anyone else knows him. Years ago, in fact, when I visited him at Auburn State prison, when he was nineteen, he said to me, "Miss Honig, you know me so well it scares me. Sometimes I think you know me better than I know myself." I agree. Willie splinters off the parts of himself that he doesn't like or doesn't want to face.

I believe that Willie's mental and emotional problems began at home in his early childhood. The only son, born between two half-sisters, without a father present, Willie was coddled and loved by his mother, sisters, aunts, and grandmother. He became the little man of the house. As he grew older and asked about his father, his mother got angry and refused to tell him anything, except that his father was a bad man and . . . you're just like your father! In this case,

Willie's high intelligence worked against him, as he was haunted by curiosity and longing to know more about this mysterious parent. It was only after the killings at age fifteen that he learned his father, Willie James Sr., was serving a life sentence for stabbing to death two men when he was twenty years old and his wife was pregnant with Willie.

Willie finally made contact with his long-lost father when he was imprisoned after the murders. To his amazement, he learned that his father had just graduated from Kansas State University and was a Phi Beta Kappa, though still serving concurrent sentences for murder and bank robbery. Father and son corresponded briefly. Soon they became estranged, however; Willie had become angry at his father's authoritarian insistence that Willie forget about the black revolution and attend to his education.

A rift developed between them and though they corresponded for a short while a few years later, Willie again ended the correspondence, rebelling against the father's renewed criticisms. When the father died in a tragic murder/suicide on March 17, 1985, after an escape attempt and a shoot-out with police, they were still estranged and had not written for over a year. Willie took his father's death without a tear. The two had never met, and so Willie was able to use it as fodder for his white racist theories. He told me his father was set up and killed by white racists who hated to see a brilliant, educated black man and wanted him dead. Untroubled by their estrangement, Willie professed to love his father and said he would fight racism to avenge him.

So the absent and then dead father, who abandoned Willie all his life, was gone, but Willie's rage persisted and escalated. Why? Willie gives obvious clues over and over again. Most of the clues are not in what he says, but in what he does not say, what he has never said, what he will never say.

Honig believes that Willie's mother is

the source of his deepest anguish, his greatest sorrow, his bottomless rage. Never will he say a word against her. She is his most faithful visitor, she has come regularly all these twelve years, despite the costs and the hardships and the precious time it has taken her away from her ailing mother, her troubled daughters, her small grandchildren who need her care. Willie keeps in close touch with her, always concerned about her, sensitive to the troubles and trauma in her hard life.

When he swallowed metal objects a couple of years ago and had to have his stomach slashed open to remove them, he showed her the fresh deep scars. Whenever he makes headlines in the New York tabloids, he knows she will read them and all her neighbors and family will be shocked and she will have to live it down, but he goes out of his way to make headlines and become a nationally known killer. Surely he knows how much suffering and sorrow he has caused her, but he never mentions it. He describes her as a loving mother who is unsophisticated, overwhelmed by family problems and unable to help him in any way but to stand by him as a mother, which she always does.

Willie is too smart to miss the point that any mother who had a son like Willie Bosket would live in constant anguish, shame, and self-recrimination, would castigate herself and try to make amends. He never mentions it. Once or twice he said he suspects some family member turned him in to the police for the subway murders, but he doesn't name the suspects. If he believes his mother betrayed him, it is much too painful to consider. Such thoughts must be pushed deep down out of his conscious mind—where they fester and boil over into the murderous rage that triggers his hideous crimes.

If his mother has committed other painful betrayals, loving other men and bringing them home, Willie ignores it or blocks it out. His older and younger half sisters, both born out of wedlock, confirm the mother's romantic liaisons, even the possibility that stepfather figures have lived in the home. If so, Willie has denied their existence, at least when he talked at length and wrote in detail to me for years. Whenever he did speak of his mother, it was on a superficial level. She was coming to visit, she worried about his younger sister, she was tending to her aged mother, she had written him, called, sent a package. She works as a security guard, looks after her grandchildren, sometimes brings nieces and a nephew to visit Willie. She was presented to me, his closest friend, as the good mother, never any less.

Schizophrenics often speak in codes or disguise the intent of their words. I find it significant that Willie Bosket tells the world over and over again that his enemy, his greatest tormentor, the one responsible for all his crimes and sorrows is "my surrogate mother, the criminal justice system." His accusations toward his surrogate mother are a repetition compulsion. He is finally able to say, to shout out loud to all the world, "My mother has destroyed me." He maintains his love/hate relationship with his real mother, protecting her and excoriating her in the same breath.

Honig describes the other family members as "shadowy."

His maternal grandmother, Nancy Spates, an intelligent woman who speaks warmly and with concern about Willie, he calls "My Heart." He speaks lovingly but seldom of her. He expresses love for his sisters, nieces, and nephew, but again, they are shadowy figures, mentioned briefly and never in depth. He speaks negatively of some family members; he calls his paternal grandmother, Marie Jackson, "The

Snake," he talked against his half sister Robin, his father's daughter, and he raged against his cousin Herman Spates for being weak and unmanly. Despite his criticisms of them, however, they too are seldom mentioned and never discussed in detail. Like most schizophrenics, Willie feels alienated from everyone. He seems to have no real family ties, no substantial connections to any other people. He lives alone, in every sense of the word. His secure, isolated confinement and the hostile prison environment can only reinforce his already deeply felt alienation toward people and the world.

Identity confusion, a schizophrenic trait, is obvious in Willie. He often rails against homosexuals and lesbians, but there is no specificity in his declamations. It seems he is making a positive statement about himself rather than a negative, sweeping indictment of homosexuals. What I think he is saying is, "I am a man, a real man." Masculinity is of utmost importance to Willie, suggesting doubts and fears. He presents a virile persona and glories in it. He describes himself as a romantic lover of women, a heartbreaker, fearless, powerful, virile, someone to be feared, respected by all—and adored by women. He has given me the impression that he is trying to convince himself and to define himself. In his progressive emotional deterioration, his ego boundaries are weakening, and by defining himself, he is trying to pull himself together. Without treatment and with time his enemy rather than his ally, he is doomed to fail.

Honig calls Willie's childhood world

a piercing disappointment, without a father, a mother with pressing romantic needs and deeds, the marginal life in Harlem, the fact that he was small for his age, living under the shadow of an evil father. As an eight-year-old, Willie set out to avenge himself against the world. Bright and alert, he quickly learned to inspire fear in people to gain their rapt attention while at the same time he could defuse his growing rage.

But rage is like blood—it regenerates almost immediately. By the time he was nine, Willie was assaulting classmates and teachers in school. By the time he was ten, his murderous rage firmly in place, he was more than his family and the community—Harlem—could tolerate. He was sent away to institutions, supposedly for treatment, but there was no treatment for anyone so angry and uncontrollable as Willie Bosket. Instead there was restraint, punishment, hostility, retaliation, and the perfect climate for the blossoming of a long, blood-curdling criminal career. Willie went in the system's gate at age ten and never came out. Now he is sentenced to spend two lifetimes locked up, probably to die in prison.

How he has remained even superficially sane all this time is a mystery to me. His ego defenses are markedly primitive. "Identification with the aggressor," a phrase of Anna Freud's, is his first line of defense. Denial and suppression are ever present: he never discusses the things that trouble him most deeply, the betrayals and ruptured family relationships. Only once since I've known Willie did he come close to revealing to me the searing emotional pain which torments him. When I failed to visit him at his demand because he was transferred hundreds of miles away to Collins Correctional Facility, he wrote me a furious "hate" letter, denouncing me for not loving him enough, just like all the other people who pretended to love him, but failed him when he needed us most. Later, he apologized for that letter, took the blame himself for his temperamental outburst and we became friends again. But for once, he gave me a glimpse of the deep sorrow in his heart.

Honig believes that

> Willie displays the basic distrust toward the world typical of a child who has never been able to rely on the consistency of parental love or the security of a protective family to shield him from an unfriendly, hurtful world. When he lashed out in anger, he was hauled into court and sent away to training schools that denied him the emotional security and nourishment he craved.
>
> Instead, his paranoid personality traits flourished and he sought relief in his own distorted perceptions of vengeance and power. By the time he was fifteen years old, Willie Bosket had made up his mind to kill or be killed. And in the dark early morning hours of March 19, 23, and 27, 1978, he went out with a Saturday night special and gunned down three people in cold blood.
>
> I believe Willie prefers to live and die in prison. I believe that horrible as this life may seem to most people, there is something far more horrible out in the world, as far as Willie Bosket is concerned. I believe that Willie lives in terror that if he is ever released, he may lose control of himself and harm or kill the person he loves the most, and possibly hates the most: his own mother. I believe Willie would rather die than commit so heinous a crime because the love he feels for his mother must still outweigh the hatred.
>
> In a May 26, 1982, letter he sent me from Auburn State Prison, nineteen-year-old Willie wrote: "I want to kill and kill and kill and kill the pigs [prison guards] until I am killed. And the only way I can be satisfied is to kill and kill the enemy . . . until I can kill no more, and that will be when I rest forever."

"Sadly, Willie will probably get his wish," Honig concludes.

* * *

For a child to mature and relate to the world with warmth, concern, and responsibility, he needs to accept the fact that all his wishes cannot be gratified pronto. He must slowly accept reality, curb pleasure. Much of growing up is learning to be at peace with the awareness the world is not a paradise or a Garden of Eden.

The first major lesson occurs when the baby is weaned. If he is warmly and patiently weaned, hugged and understood, comforted when he becomes frustrated and cries, the setting of limits does not become a painful, angry experience. But if a baby is arbitrarily and coldly weaned, he begins to believe all frustrations are perpetrated by hostile persons. He may become quite paranoid, filled with hate. To be able to care for others requires that we first be cared for. The infant who was not weaned warmly and tenderly is full of rage. He wants to deprive others as he feels deprived. One of the coldest killers now behind bars, Charles Manson, grew up with a mother who was a prostitute, had little time for him and no doubt wished he had never been born.

Just as there are parents who angrily wean their infants and also treat the child with rage, there are also parents who cannot tolerate a moment of their infant's anger and frustration and indulge the child freely and lavishly, in some cases for many years.

These parents have not learned the value of an occasional "no." If a child gets everything he wants, all his wishes fulfilled immediately, he will not develop that tolerance of frustration we all need to successfully accept life and its limitations. Such a chid is likely to become violent whenever someone tries to set limits for him.

The child who has been indulged and overgratified is a potential murderer, for he feels he has the right to yell and scream, hit and smash, when someone does not give him at once what he demands. The "nos," however, should not be administered to a baby or child in a harsh, hateful tone but a quiet, understanding one that conveys the feeling

"Life at times has to be painful—you will not get your every wish fulfilled."

If a child has been warmly fed and kindly weaned, he will be able to progress easily from one level of development to the next. He starts to derive satisfaction from mastering his wishes and increasing his range of experience with others. It is difficult for any child to mature, because maturity implies accepting frustrations. The baby who has lived a life of consistent and constant gratification is not eager to change.

When anybody has been the recipient of bounties, it takes courage not to feel angry at deprivation. All babies must move from being a receiver to becoming a giver. When babies start to be toilet-trained, they often view their feces as "gifts" to the parent. However, no baby wants to bestow a gift if he is prematurely toilet-trained. This training should not start as a rule until the middle of the second year of life.

Many of the power struggles between adults, such as exist in marriage and at work, are a reliving of the hatred the person felt as a child when toilet-trained. Many a furious spouse or lover sees his partner as the parent of childhood making him "take a shit right now!" Power struggles, when intense, lead to violence similar to the violence mothers or fathers feel toward uncooperative children and similar to the violence children feel toward parents who are cruel and sadistic.

Many an adult hates to work, hates to relate to others, hates to obey rules of any kind, feels at times violent and murderous. This is the child within who has been made "to make" prematurely, arbitrarily, and hostilely. Such a child feels deeply misunderstood, not cared for. He often grows up without ever enjoying childhood. The seeds are laid out for him to become an irresponsible, uncaring, heartless person—perhaps a murderer.

It is often asked, "Is every murderer someone who was treated violently as a child?" The answer is no. As we have already suggested, some children turn out to be violent adults and, in some cases, actual murderers who were not abused or rejected but indulged and overgratified. They became egocentric, impulsive, and hostile if they did not get their own way.

When a child is not given limits, guidance, and controls, he feels an inalienable right to continue demanding what he wants at the moment. This may be the child weaned very late in life. Or the child toilet-trained very late in life. Or the child who feels that he is His Royal Highness the Prince—the world is his oyster and all he has to concern himself with are his own selfish wishes.

All children—and, for that matter, all adults—yearn to be princes or princesses with no responsibilities other than to gratify themselves. Yet all children and all adults, if they are to work and love enjoyably and productively, have to learn to monitor their egocentric wishes.

If a child has never been trained to accept no for an answer, he fights constantly with his siblings, enters into the neighborhood unable to share with his peers, and is hostile toward every rule and regulation at school. If he feels cooperation, responsibility, and caring for others are cruel indignities imposed on him, he may even become a murderer when he does not get his own way.

We might say that the child who has not learned to accept the fact that there are others in this world besides himself has been neglected. But the neglect is of a different kind than usually described. The neglect the parents of such a youngster show comes from their failure to help the child tame his wishes, control his desires, and empathize with others.

Often the parents of such a youngster have been brutalized, suffering from their sadistic and arbitrary parental handling when they were children. To cope with these resentments, they keep their children "babies" as they vicariously spite their parents.

The child we are talking about is a Peter Pan who says, "I won't grow up, I won't grow up." He is aided and abetted by parents who feel uncomfortable in imposing limits and structure. The parent is frightened of being the recipient of the child's inevitable anger when the parent imposes limits or guidance. Rather than cope with the child's inevitable anger at restrictions, the parent will indulgently neglect any supervision. To face the child's anger is to be reminded of the parent's childhood anger, which he does not want to admit.

One couple visited friends who had a two-year-old they had never seen before. They were shaken to observe that the child ruled the household. The parents did not thwart one of his wishes, allowed him to order their day, eat what he wished, do what he wished. The slightest rise in his voice brought them to his side to soothe him.

Riding home, the wife turned to her husband and correctly stated, "They are creating a monster in that child. He will never be satisfied with anything. I predict he will be a very angry person."

The very narcissistic child, who may become a delinquent, later a criminal, and perhaps eventually a murderer, is a furious baby saying to the world, "I must have my every wish come true pronto. If you don't gratify my wishes at once, I will kill you!" This angry, violent behavior is what the schizophrenic youngster or adult who withdraws into his world of delusions and hallucinations defends against.

The schizophrenic child holds back his anger at being abused. Instead, he idealizes his parents as he makes himself the sinner. Occasionally the schizophrenic child or adolescent cannot contain his rage. He turns it away from himself and may act violently.

Many of those who commit murder are treated callously or indifferently, or abused in their early life. They never dared discharge hostile aggression against a parent but later felt free to hate someone symbolically experienced as the cruel parent. Joseph Kallinger is a striking example of a child who was severely abused and became an abuser. And although we do not know all the details of John

Hinckley's life, he received much indulgence but few controls and might be considered the would-be murderer who never learned to accept realistic limits. To understand a murderer, we have to know much about his early life and the way his parents treated him.

Very often a violent adult and occasionally a murderous adult was a child who had to grow up too fast. He was forced to master weaning too early, obliged to take no for an answer too soon, and often became a little adult at three or four. This same child often served as parent to his own parents. Usually he was not aware of the frustration and rage he felt when he could not enjoy the pleasures of childhood.

As an adult he may be a hard-working, compulsive person who, after taking care of so many people so much of the time, explodes and throws the temper tantrums he wanted to exhibit for many years but did not dare.

As the child gradually resolves the conflict between the urge to express his instinctual wishes and the desire to maintain the security of his relationship with his parents by conforming to their demands, he becomes less narcissistic. About the age of three a child should begin to bestow loving feelings as well as receive them.

Initially, children love both parents indiscriminately but between the ages of three and six they turn their affection with greater intensity to the parent of the opposite sex and compete with the parent of the same sex.

Although there is ongoing debate among psychologists and social scientists as to whether this is a biological phenomenon or evolves because of the way the family is constituted and society conducts interpersonal arrangements, the evidence is clear that all children in all cultures turn their love with greater intensity to the parent of the opposite sex and compete with the parent of the same sex.

The anthropologist Bronislaw Malinowski, who studied family patterns in many different cultures, concluded that the conflict is universal. The three-year-old boy starts to notice his father loving his mother and inevitably wants the privileges and pleasures his father receives from his mother. The girl makes similar observations and inevitably desires from her father what her mother receives—love, hugs, attention and a bedroom for just the two of them.

The competition the three-year-old feels with the parent of the same sex exists also in one-parent families. Even if the child has never seen a mother with a father, he is aware of the available one parent interacting with members of the opposite sex and inevitably wants to compete.

There are profound difficulties for children in one-parent families. Even in one-parent homes children compete with absent parents, uncles, aunts, or imaginary parents. Researchers in child development have discovered the fascinating finding that all children, regardless of family composition, picture themselves in fantasy and dreams with a father and mother and, depending on their sex, compete with one and try to possess the other.

If the relationship between mother and father is a loving and cooperative one, in which the child sees a minimum of hatred, the wish to compete is not an intense one. But, as we know in our society and most societies, it is the rare family in which the mother and father are consistently observed loving each other, cooperating with each other, enjoying both each other and their own children.

Many married couples handle their hatred by demeaning their partners in front of their children. Frequently this is done subtly, as when the father says to his daughter, "Your mother is so forgetful." But often it is carried out with derision, as when a mother says to her son in contempt, "Your father is an abysmal failure in his business," be he a Wall Street broker or owner of a small restaurant.

Regardless of the family atmosphere, whether loving or hateful or, as in most instances, when love and hate take turns, the child's conflicts at the age of three to five are not easy to resolve. Some psychologists wonder whether anyone ever fully resolves the wish to compete with and surpass the parent of the same sex. The resolution perhaps is always a matter of degree.

This dilemma, referred to as the Oedipal conflict, is difficult to resolve because no matter how ambitious and determined children are, it is highly unusual for a small child, girl or boy, to emerge a victor over an adult twice or three times his size and, perhaps of greater importance, someone whom the child needs to get along in life. As much as a young girl may want to wipe out her mother and be alone with Daddy, she needs her mother to survive emotionally.

This conflict is observed in many areas of living; we will discuss it as it emerges in work, politics, sports, and marriage. But we now consider how the Oedipal conflict can sow the seeds of murder.

If a boy, while normally competitive with his father, is demeaned and derogated by the father as he tries to surpass him—by becoming a Superman or a David who wishes to slay Goliath or a Jack in the Beanstalk who yearns to grow taller than any father in the world—then the boy feels intense rage toward the father for attacking him. If a boy's normal competitiveness is not accepted by his father, who instead is critical and tears him down, the boy will feel that anyone who shows more strength and competence than he is an enemy too.

If a boy's father is not successful in his work, the boy often feel guilty in surpassing his father. Such a boy can never enjoy success but must think of himself as a failure regardless of his achievements. In his mind, if he achieves he feels he is supplanting his father, which he believes sinful.

Many a person who constantly fails cannot enjoy success, believes he has committed an imaginary crime—a crime of weakening or destroying the parent of the same sex. Feeling he must fail, he becomes depressed and apathetic. In extreme cases he feels homicidal or suicidal. While he thinks of murdering others or himself for feeling like a colossal failure, he actually is guilty about his success.

While no one is completely exempt from angry thoughts, the more the father cannot tolerate his son's wishes to surpass him, the angrier the boy becomes, the more revengeful he feels, and the more likely he is to pick a fight with everyone he encounters. The fighting may be limited to arguments as the rivals try to humiliate each other verbally. Or it may be extended to physical fights or, in extreme cases, actual murder.

Many a murder involves one man competing with another for the symbolic woman. "She" may be turf in gang warfare, the prize in an athletic contest, such as the heavyweight championship, or land or power in countries that wage war on each other.

When John Hinkley tried to kill President Reagan because he fantasized that the President kept Jodie Foster, the actress, away from him, every man, woman, and adolescent took an interest in the case. We are all to some extent John Hinkleys who want the beautiful mother, or, if we are girls, the handsome father.

The more hatred we experienced in our families, the more competitive we felt toward parents of the same sex, the more we identify with a John Hinkley. Those who can acknowledge their competitiveness as part of being human are a little less revengeful toward a Hinckley. They are not so furious that he is treated in a mental hospital rather than getting a lifelong sentence in prison.

Those who cannot tolerate their competitive wishes see them as something foreign. They feel punitive toward a Hinckley, want him incarcerated for life, out of their minds, their own desires denied. Frequently the more punitive we feel toward an asocial act, the more we want to punish ourselves at the thought of doing the same. This is one reason few people really feel compassion for or try to understand a murderer. His act stirs the murderous, competitive wishes within all of us.

Perhaps one of the main factors in violent behavior that

turns murderous is that the perpetrator feels like a three- or four-year-old child next to a powerful parental figure he envies and who threatens him. Many a man or woman commits murder because the perpetrator feels so weak next to someone so strong and cannot tolerate the feelings of threat, vulnerability, and deprivation compared to "the big shot"—the person he wants to shoot.

If parents are understanding—if they respect and love each other, work together, love and protect the child—the mature boy or girl will be inclined to sing the familiar song "I want a girl [or boy] just like the girl [or boy] who married dear old Dad [or Mom]."

But if parents are competitive with each other, angry at each other, uncooperative, always in power struggles, the child emerges more and more as a hostile competitor who can become quite capable of destructive behavior. A woman of twenty-six who stabbed her husband to death when he threatened to walk out on her told the officer who arrested her, "I saw my mother kill my father when I was ten and he said he was going to leave both of us for another woman, one he loved more. It seemed the natural thing for me to do when I felt furious caught in the same predicament years later."

It is the rare child who later in life as an adult cannot outdo the parent, when it comes to hatred and the wish to destroy.

Around the age of six or seven, most children tend to renounce the family romance and move toward friendship with children of the same sex. Concomitantly, a move occurs toward closeness with the parent of the same sex. Children reason, "If I can't lick 'em, I'll join 'em." Boys between six and ten move closer to their fathers, while girls do the same with their mothers.

Although this is changing somewhat, particularly in suburban communities, children at this age spend most of their time with peers of the same gender, joining Little League baseball teams, Cub Scouts, or Brownies.

The reason children in their preteens seek peers of the same gender is that they are afraid of their own sexuality. As our society moves toward recognizing the power of the sexual feeling in all children, there are fewer taboos against boys and girls playing with each other and less anxiety about this emerging into sexual play.

While the move toward the parent of the same sex and peers of the same sex should be regarded as a normal, healthy development, many boys and girls stay fixed at this position. Never or rarely do they move out toward the opposite sex. There is much controversy on this issue, and psychologists and psychiatrists who have worked with children and their parents point out that those who tend to rely exclusively for pleasure in relationships with members of their own sex are those who found the competition frightening and threatening between themselves and the parent of the same sex.

Many a man who feels he cannot assert himself with his male boss and many a woman who cannot do the same with a female supervisor in many ways feels like a nine- or ten-year-old child fearful of competing with a father or mother.

It is rarely easy for a frightened person who feels obliged to inhibit normal aggressive feelings toward another adult to face himself. When we feel to some extent intimidated by an authoritarian boss, we may ascribe our fears to the job situation or to the boss. Unsympathetic, dictatorlike bosses and arbitrary, insensitive superiors exist everywhere. When we become obsessed with them, too frightened to figure out reasonable ways to cope with them that do not put us in jeopardy, we are like children standing before mammoth parents. We do not permit ourselves to feel or use our realistic strengths.

A thirty-two-year-old man who we will call Sam Snyder was a brilliant computer analyst with many skills and much training. He worked in a large firm, but he was never promoted, despite his efficiency and effectiveness. A silent man, Sam was not noticed by anyone. The more he was ignored and overlooked, the more others surpassed him in salary and rank, the more depressed he became. He started to suffer severe heart spasms and developed an ulcer. It was not until he went into therapy that he realized how frightened he felt about asserting himself, acting on his own behalf, because he knew if he did say anything, all the hatred he felt toward his superiors would emerge and he would scream and curse them. This was the way he had wanted to act as a boy and man toward his restrictive and authoritarian father but never could.

If we do not acknowledge that we turn someone into the feared father or mother of our past, we start to feel more anxious, more threatened, more irritable. Believing we are weak and vulnerable, obliged to submit for long periods of time, our violence may eventually erupt.

In the preceding chapter we discussed some of the Presidential assassins. All of these men psychologically experienced themselves as little boys competing with "big daddies." In their fantasies, the murderers or would-be murderers tried to cajole, manipulate, and win over the "daddies." But like those who believe they must submit for long periods of time to "bosses," they eventually exploded in the built-up rage that led to murder.

One of the major factors in overt murder is that the perpetrator feels like a submissive child forced to be a slave too long. This may be the main reason why members of minority groups such as blacks or Hispanics and perhaps Jews at certain times in history became so murderous. When Jewish people at Passover celebrate the vanquishing of the Pharaohs in Egypt, they say at the Seder service, "We were slaves under the Pharaohs and we will not permit that to happen again."

If the discomfort toward the parent of the opposite sex remains high, then gangs and groups of one's own gender replace home and family. Many boys who live with only a mother join gangs that have proliferated and obviously provide a haven for the growing boy who cannot rely on a father to offer protection against his growing, frightening sexuality. The groups that form when members are ten or eleven often become the murderous gangs of adolescence.

When a child is in a power struggle with the parent of the same sex, this discomfort will emerge in later relationships with adults experienced as mother figures to women, or father figures to men. In the earlier example of Sam Snyder his discomfort with his father continually re-emerged with bosses.

We cannot examine the seeds of murder that develop in childhood without noting the importance of brothers and sisters to each other. Siblings are often used to express much of the competition, envy, and rivalry for the parents. Many a girl would rather hate her sister than compete with her mother. Many a boy would rather hate his brother than compete with his father.

The hostility so frequently exhibited toward parents is expressed much more freely toward brothers and sisters. Experts on child care and development know that when siblings are engaged in deep rivalry, this rivalry often expresses a disguised displacement of hatred toward parents.

Brothers and sisters also fight to ward off sexual fantasies toward each other. Siblings of the same sex, frightened of warm or sexual feelings, may fight verbally or physically to escape the discomfort of feeling too close. The underlying relationship with siblings is frequently negative because all siblings to some extent are rivals for the parents' love. As one four-year-old girl exclaimed, looking at the new baby in the crib, "Mommy, how could you do this to me?"

An eight-year-old girl was aghast one spring day when her ten-year-old brother stuffed a small, wriggly worm down her back. She complained to her mother, "How could Peter dare do that to me?" Years later, when she went into psychoanalysis, she told the analyst of her horror that day. He explained that her brother was undoubtedly stirred sexually and the worm represented his penis in a disguised fashion.

The more a child feels deprived of love and is convinced that someone else, such as a sibling, is receiving
what he needs, rage and fantasies are inevitable. Inasmuch
as every child who has a brother or sister is forced to share
the parents' attention, love, and concern, every child who
has a sibling inevitably becomes a rival of that sibling. In
some instances, if the family atmosphere is a hostile one
and the love of the parent often is in doubt, the rivalry can
reach violent proportions. A sibling can become at least in
fantasy a little Hitler who wants his brother or sister (or
both) out of the way.

Thus, within every adult there exists a child hungry for
attention and love, who wants all his parents' attention and
love. Sharing, cooperating, empathizing with a rival are
adult traits that take work and often arduous effort. Inasmuch as all of us are children at heart to some degree, we
are all capable of rivalry and hatred toward anyone who
has something we lack, whether it be money, status,
power, possessions, or love.

The more we feel like the deprived, angry little child,
the more we want to see others deprived. If our feelings of
deprivation, whether real or imagined, are intense, we may
go so far as wishing to deprive the other person of his life.
Irrationality in adulthood is real because our wishes and
desires from childhood still seem strong and real.

Because the child in all of us never completely disap-
pears and wants his every wish fulfilled and pronto, rivalry, competition, and violence exist in all cultures. A
joke popular in Russia is about Ivan, who owns a goat,
and Boris, who does not, an injustice Boris bitterly resents.
One night Boris is visited by his guardian angel. "I see
your problem," the angel says, "and now I'll give you
what you want." Boris cheers up and asks, "You mean
you're going to kill Ivan's goat?"

Boris in Russia is no different from John in America or
Marie in France. When the other person possesses what
we want, we all see red. Red for blood.

* * *

One final, important observation may be made about the seeds of murder in the baby and child. At this time in our culture childhood is not always safe. More children than ever live on the streets or in families shattered by divorce, drugs, or poverty. Mounting economic pressures have squeezed the middle class so that a 1989 Congressional study concluded, "Childhood has become far more precarious and less safe for millions of America's children."

Even for children who seem destined for high achievement, hopes appear tempered as the drug culture, the decline of the nuclear family, and the decline of many excellent schools appear overwhelming.

As more and more children live in one-parent families, violence takes a heavier toll. This is particularly true among black youngsters who do not experience two parents loving each other and working together in their behalf.

As suggested earlier, hatred, violence, and murder can never be divorced from the culture in which they take place. Our culture still remains a "hate" culture in which parents find it difficult to consistently love each other and their children. This ugly but true state of family affairs produces the seeds for many murders.

It is important to keep in mind that in the 1990s as the number of killings soars in big cities across the United States and as violence in all its forms reaches an all-time high, the nuclear family is more fractured, spouses are more full of hate, and emotional happiness seems more difficult, if not impossible, for many men and women.

4

Murder in Adolescence

Adolescence is "an interruption in peaceful growth," in the words of the late Anna Freud, who worked with teenagers.

Central Park in Manhattan is one of the most beautiful places in the world as spring wafts into New York City. But on April 19, 1989, one of the first warm evenings of the year, as a nearly full moon shone in a clear sky, the park turned into one of the most horrifying spots on the globe.

The next day, seven youths from Harlem were charged with a savage attack on a twenty-eight-year-old white woman jogger, whom they left for dead in a ravine near the 102nd Street transverse. Earlier they had attacked a white man whom they also left for dead, and threatened to attack others jogging in the park.

The youths, later known as the "wilding" pack, had entered the park from Harlem and made their way down its east side, where they attacked a male jogger. Then they went in search of more prey, their appetites whetted.

It was almost ten o'clock at night and the park was practically deserted. Suddenly on the west side they saw the woman jogger (her name was never disclosed, for this was a rape case), running by herself. She was of medium

73

height, thin, with close-cropped brown hair. She wore black biking pants, gray shorts, a long-sleeved white shirt, and Saucony running shoes.

According to Richardson Clarence Thomas, who told this to the police, one of the boys, Antron McCray, pushed the jogger to the ground while others "hit and kicked her." She was screaming, "Stop! Stop! Get off me!"

Michael Briscoe, another of the boys, punched her repeatedly (he later claimed he left the park earlier and was not indicted for the rape). Yusef Salaam hit her on the head with a metal pipe he was carrying and she fell down. Whereupon he struck her again, later telling the police, "because it was fun." The gang then dragged her off the roadway to a small slope in a wooded area and, according to Thomas, took her clothes off. Raymond Santana pinned her arms to the ground. Steve Lopez held her legs, shouting, "Shut up, bitch!"

Several of the boys then raped her and she was hit again on the head with the pipe before they left her bleeding to death on the slope. One also said he smashed a broken brick into her face. An investigator later reported that at least four boys had intercourse with her and one sodomized her. She was left sprawled across the roots of a budding maple tree as the boys fled through the woods toward the west boundary of the park.

Thomas told police they were laughing, leaping, and cavorting as they flung the victim's clothes as far as eighty feet from the site of the rape. Left for dead, blood seeping out of her body, the woman survived because at 1:30 A.M. two men, walking through the park, saw her body, naked except for a jogging bra. Her hands were under her chin clutching her blood-soaked shirt.

The two men called the police, who took her to Metropolitan Hospital, where Dr. Robert Kurtz, head of surgical intensive care, said she had lost three-fourths of her blood and a blockage in her throat obstructed her breathing. He predicted that within the hour she "almost certainly would be dead."

She was identified later that morning by two co-workers at Salomon Brothers, the Wall Street investment company, after they linked her absence at work to news reports of the rape. She suffered multiple skull fractures, her face was swollen and bruised, she had cuts from a knife and bruises on her chest, arms, legs, hands, and feet. Her simple gold ring was the only way she could be identified.

Not expected to live, somehow she possessed the strength to survive. Slowly she regained her senses though she would not remember the gory details of that terrifying night. She suffered continuing brain damage and needed long rehabilitation.

In reconstructing the crime and the lives of the accused assailants, each one showed a history of acute family instability, problems in school, difficulty in relationships from birth to adolescence, and severe disciplinary conflicts. Most had school records of failures in their studies. There were no fathers in most of the homes.

According to *The New York Times,* Raymond Santana, fourteen, in the eighth grade at the Key School, a program for slow learners in East Harlem, lived with his grandmother and father on East 119th Street. Law enforcement officials described him as a "known troublemaker" and the ringleader of the Central Park attacks. One of his teachers called the father "an absent father" and described his treatment of his son as "total neglect."

As a child Raymond grew up on University Avenue in the Bronx with his mother, whom he is reported to have said he "hated." School officials described his home as the scene of drugs, drinking, and promiscuity. One teacher commented, "This kid was thrown out of the cradle. He was cheated out of his mother's nurturing from day one." He had recently told a friend that his mother was "dead." His teacher said he had stopped taking part in sports.

The vicious attack on the jogger aroused more reaction in the press and public than most rapes and near murders in New York. Mayor Koch called the boys "monsters." Donald Trump took out advertisements in several newspapers demanding the return of the death penalty. The *New York Post* of April 24, 1989, headlined news of the attack "City of Shame: Rape Shows No One in Town Is Safe." Tom Wicker, in his column in *The New York Times* of April 28, said of those who believed the victim had no business being in the park after dark, "Indeed, the woman assaulted in the park by a gang of 'wilding' teenagers had every right to be where she was at that time. If, because of the fear that afflicts most urban dwellers, she had shied from running there, she would have surrendered to that fear and yielded her freedom to those who caused it, as most of us do."

He went on, "Instead, she affirmed the primacy of freedom over fear; all honor to her for that." He called the crime "inexplicable," said the attackers were "surely influenced by the social pathologies of the inner city," in which they lived, one that "still separates blacks and whites in this country."

There is nothing more abhorrent than to learn that an innocent victim, woman or man, has been brutalized, raped, and sodomized. It stirs in all of us an outrage that leads to intense wishes for revenge and violent moral indignation. We identify with the innocent woman jogger struck unconscious by a heavy metal pipe, held down by her attackers as some raped her, then left for dead. We want to murder the murderers.

We all are vulnerable to such attacks and thus cry out, "Kill the killers!" But what of the adolescents who committed these savage atrocities on the young woman jogger and others in the park that night? What motivated their savagery?

As we learn from reading the records of their backgrounds, they came from broken or severely unhappy homes. All were either black or Hispanic. All had histories of abuse, physical or mental or both, by parents. All apparently felt the white majority were their enemies, that they were a vulnerable, put-down minority.

Like a pack of angry wolves, the gang did to the jogger

what they had experienced or seen or heard about during the course of their earlier lives, as they, in turn, acted cruelly and wildly. But we cannot be satisfied with that explanation alone. We need to explore further *why* so many teenagers, white as well as black, commit murders. Teenagers from wealthy white homes and middle-class white families also kill, not only strangers but parents or siblings, as our daily newspapers attest.

Statistics reveal that a high percentage of murders of all kinds, rapes, and violent attacks are perpetrated by teenagers from both minority and majority groups. Not long after the attack on the jogger, one of the authors of this book was walking along Fifty-eighth Street and Seventh Avenue past five black youths in their late teens. One said loudly to another, so that passersby could clearly hear, "It's either fuck or fight, I tell 'em." Then angrily, "I say to a girl, 'I don't have a hard-on for nothing.' " This most certainly shows the lack of feeling for a member of the opposite sex. No doubt they transfer to young women the same scorn they saw their fathers or other men show for their mothers.

Let us look first at the nature of adolescence. Why do many adolescents act impulsively and cruelly? Since the beginning of recorded time, adolescents have baffled and astounded us. Literary portrayals of teenagers have abounded. Romeo and Juliet poignantly depicted teenage passion. Shakespeare's Prince Hal shows an adolescent terrified by his sexual stirrings.

In our own century, James Joyce, Thomas Mann, William Faulkner, Tennessee Williams, and many others have continued the literary tradition of sexual conflicts, turmoil, and unpredictable actions in teenagers and young men and women.

Some of the typical characteristics—jumpiness, sexual excitement, intense narcissism, and acute self-doubts—are revealed in the following passage from J. D. Salinger's *Catcher in the Rye:*

I apologized like a madman because the band was starting a fast one. She started jitterbugging with me—but just very nice and easy, not corny. She was really good. All you had to do was touch her and when she turned around her pretty little butt twitched so nice and all. She knocked me out, I mean it. I was about half in love with her by the time we sat down. That's the thing about girls. Every time they do something pretty, even if they're sort of stupid, you fall half in love with them and then you never know where the hell you are.

Like Holden Caulfield, the adolescent portrayed in Salinger's book, the teenager can go from the height of elation to the depths of despair in a single hour. He can feel enthusiasm one day, hopelessness the next. Frequently believing he is oppressed by parents and other older persons, as he struggles to establish a sense of identity the adolescent loudly proclaims, "I rebel, therefore I am!"

One of the reasons the teenage years are so agonizing is that in most societies, particularly ours, the adolescent is emotionally neither fish nor fowl. On the one hand, he still wants to be loved and coddled like a child but he also wants to be independent and emancipated from his parents.

Most teenagers ride an emotional seesaw. One day they wish to be a superadult, the next day they wish to regress to the status of childhood. The teenager shows considerable volatility of feelings. There seems no consistency in the young person's love or hate, interest or boredom: each emotion grips the teenager totally, though not for long.

Because the teenager is an intensely emotional person, swamped by the fantasies and wishes puberty creates, he often becomes very impulsive and shows poor judgment. Adolescence, by definition, may be referred to as "an interruption in peaceful growth," in the words of one of the world's foremost experts on adolescence, the late Anna Freud, who worked with teenagers. She wrote:

It is normal for an adolescent to behave for a considerable length of time in an inconsistent and unpredictable manner, to fight impulses and to accept them; to ward them off successfully and to be overrun by them; to love his parents and to hate them; to revolt against them and to be dependent on them; to be deeply ashamed to acknowledge his mother before others, and unexpectedly to desire heart-to-heart talks with her; to thrive on imitation of and identification with others while searching unceasingly for his own identity; to be more idealistic, artistic, generous and unselfish than he will ever be again but also the opposite—self-centered, egotistic, calculating. Such fluctuations between extreme opposites would be deemed highly abnormal at any other time of life.

The adolescent who fluctuates in mood, activity, and interests is forever assuming new values. He is invariably engaged in an activity that can be called "bribing his conscience." He vows not to go "all the way sexually," then punishes himself severely when he does.

He pets above the waist but not below. He does not have too much sex on the first date but permits it on the second. These compromises are an attempt to appease a growing conscience and to assuage guilt feelings. For a while the teenager may become a rigid celibate and recluse, then follow this modus vivendi by indulging in extreme forms of sexual promiscuity. The young man may experiment with homosexuality, then turn into a Don Juan as though to deny his homosexual escapades.

Sexual impulses of all kinds terrify many teenagers. Some try to escape all feelings, then are depressed when they do not gratify the intense desires that are natural at this time of life.

When sexuality bombards the naive teenager, he often feels overwhelmed but attributes his acute discomfort to the environment. This is why so many teenagers run away from home and from school. They believe, as most of us tend to do, that their discomfort is caused by their environment, meaning their parents' behavior.

One of the features of teenage years insufficiently recognized is that the teenager relives his childhood over and over. All the struggles he experienced earlier in life reemerge emotionally, in fantasy. If the teenager was not helped to gain a sense of trust in himself and his parents in the first year of life, distrust of himself and everyone else will become more acute during adolescence.

Most teenagers also experience deep conflicts about food. One day they hoard it, the next they abstain from it. To deny their dependency on the mother who provides food, they concoct their own peculiar preferences and food mixes, such as peanut-butter-and-salami sandwiches, or pizza with yogurt, and frequent vegetarianism, ignoring meat as though it were poison.

If they engaged in lengthy power struggles with parents during their "terrible twos," such struggles will be intensified in adolescence. All their revived rebellion against controls emerges in their use of foul language and disregard of appropriate clothes and cleanliness. They feel guilty about rebelling against rules and regulations, so that one day they wear dirty jeans, then don a tuxedo or an evening gown for a party.

If the teenager had early difficulty in accepting sexual fantasies toward the parent of the opposite sex and competitive fantasies toward the parent of the same sex, sexuality may become a ticklish problem. Sexual feelings create anxiety in every teenager as he experiences heightened body stimulation. If sex was taboo in growing up, he may work overtime to deny his feelings as he faces more intense natural excitement than in earlier years.

When a boy is five and his mother says, "Don't touch yourself," he may repress his sexual feelings without too much of a cost to his psychological welfare. But at fifteen, when he feels a far more intense arousal, he finds it extremely difficult to acquiesce to his parents' "no-no."

Often overlooked, not only with teenagers but adults too, are the earlier "forbiddens" that remain within us. This explains why so many teenagers and adults reject full sexuality—they are still driven by the "nos" and "shouldn'ts" of childhood.

If we understand the teenager as a child with intense conflicts felt more acutely than ever, some of which may even have caused the teenager to become a murderer, seeming enigmas start to become clear.

The famous Chicago Leopold and Loeb murder in the 1930s, committed by two teenagers, who brutally and deliberately killed a younger boy, can be partially or at least hypothetically explained by the fact that both young men in fantasy were murdering a younger sibling they had wished exterminated during childhood. They felt even more acutely murderous during the teenage years.

Many a young man, troubled by feelings of sexual incompetence as he views an older sister or a mother, feels so humiliated that to prove himself a man, he fantasies he is a sexual superman. During adolescence he feels his incompetence acutely and his sexuality intensely. He may even commit rape to show he is a man, though rape holds anger as well as the need for sexual outlet.

In one-parent families where a boy lives alone with his mother, he may harbor a deep guilt that increases as his sexual fantasies about his mother become more intense and there is no father on the scene to help him monitor his desire. He fears the danger of becoming his mother's lover, with no man present to stop him.

If sexual desires toward a parent are burgeoning and there is no limiting control on the child, as when a boy lives alone with his mother for many years, to cope with this difficult situation he may turn to other boys or men and become "buddies," sometimes sexual buddies.

It is more than a coincidence that all-male gangs proliferate in neighborhoods where boys live alone with a mother and there is no father to protect them. These gangs, if one listens to them talk to each other, have a favorite word—"motherfucker." Black boys say "motherfucker" more than any other word, it would appear, as you walk down almost any street in New York and hear blacks throw out the word interminably.

All except one of the boys who raped the jogger were fatherless and sanctioned each other as they raped an older woman—a mother figure. The twenty-eight-year-old jogger was alone, without a man to protect her, as were most of the mothers of the attackers. Their homes lacked a man and the emotional brakes he would supply against intense adolescent sexual wishes.

How does a young boy feel toward a mature woman who is sexually stimulating? Particularly a woman such as the jogger, who wore skin-tight black biking pants. He feels stimulated but weak, since she is both enticing and taboo—she belongs to somebody else. But he desires her sexually, as in fantasy he does his mother. He may cope with this intense feeling through violent behavior—rape. Violence is his way of saying, I am *not* small and impotent, I am not weak, you do not dominate me, I can dominate you now.

Another major issue in the rape of the jogger is that the young men joined with each other in the brutal physical attack and rape and therefore saw each other's genitals. This turned the rape into what often occurs in a locker room—young men peering at each other's naked bodies, particularly the penis.

Perhaps another reason for the indignation many felt as they heard of the violent rape in the park is because it stirred in them their own feelings of sexual incompetency, their own rage at those who stimulated them as children but made sex seem taboo as they grew up. By condemning a minority group that acted out all our forbidden wishes, we find a small outlet for our wish to join members of our own sex in some kind of sexually violent excitement perpetrated on a member of the opposite sex.

It is important, whenever we condemn someone, to look at the behavior we condemn. Frequently the behavior symbolizes our most forbidden wishes. The vice crusader as he reflects about the horror of vice gets forbidden pleasure out of his ruminations. The compulsive housecleaner thinks about the forbidden dirt she consciously abhors but unconsciously enjoys wallowing in, like little children do about forbidden playing in the mud. When we become preoccupied with a violent rape we also gratify forbidden wishes to brutalize and be brutalized.

Few acknowledge this in ourselves because we want to keep our murderous wishes, our violent wishes, our sexual wishes, far away from our conscious desires. One way to achieve this emotional distance is to wipe out those who commit the very deeds that fascinate us but which we repudiate.

Rather than understand, for instance, what drove the "wilding" gang to act so ferociously, many of us shared Trump's view—give them the death penalty, murder the murderers. In this way we discharged our own murderous wishes but for a "good" cause. Thus we do not become aware of the part in all of us that has strong sexual fantasies toward a mother or father, as well as conflicts about parents, and heterosexual and homosexual wishes.

It is far easier to verbally attack the rapist, murder the killer, than to face our inner wishes to rape and murder and realize that their power comes from earlier relationships with parents who have intentionally or unintentionally been cruel and violent toward us at times.

Very often the dilemmas of the teenager are intensified by his parents. In many ways he is accepted by his mother and father as a maturing preadult but in other ways he is also infantilized. The teenager may obtain permission to stay out late, attend parties and dances, handle his own money, assume more responsibility for leisure time, choose his friends, and solve some of his problems. Yet many parents, frightened by the instability the teenager often shows, inhibit him in situations where freedom formerly was given.

Though he is encouraged to date, he is often forced to abide by an arbitrary time to return home. This implies he is not capable of deciding when he is tired and needs sleep. Although many parents wish to feel relatively relaxed about their children's friends, they restrict their teenager's choice of friendships. They try to exert more control than the teenager needs.

Often the social life of a teenage girl is tightly controlled by her parents. They project their own sexual anxieties onto the daughter's dating scene, and by controlling her activities temporarily reduce their own anxiety.

This is true not only of daughters. A mother warned her sixteen-year-old son, who was dating a girl in his class, when he brought her home for supper, "Be careful of her. I sense something I don't trust."

"What do you mean, Mother?" he asked.

"The way she flirts with your younger brother. Like she has to be the star in everybody's life."

"That's because she's friendly to everyone."

"I just don't trust her!" the mother repeated emphatically.

Though psychologists and other experts have talked and written about the ambivalence of adolescence, little has been said about the adult world's ambivalence toward the teenager. Parents are loath to let go of their beloved child, no matter how difficult their offspring has been at times over the years. While most parents wish to see their teenagers grow up and become independent and productive, they also want to keep their children dependent and clinging.

On the one hand we have a tendency to idealize the teenager. Adults admire and envy his romantic interests, passionate attachments, rebellions, and provocative outbursts. But unconsciously most adults are jealous of the teenager's burgeoning sexuality and find it difficult to cope with their own reactions.

Some mothers and fathers use teenagers as their role models. The teenager sets the tone for the length of hair and hairstyles, clothes, and even political and social interests. On the other hand, the teenagers' passions and sexuality frighten many adults (as they recall their frightened parents when they were teenagers). Often the tendency exists to become more restrictive than necessary.

This restrictiveness, when excessive, induces deep rage in the adolescent. His rage can assume many forms, including the accusation that the parent is "old-fashioned," "out of sync with modern morals," "a fuddy-duddy."

Such rage may induce violent reactions, even murder, in the teenager. Recently an adopted son murdered his mother and father when they refused to let him, a white youth, bring his girlfriend, a black, into the house. He had managed for weeks to sneak her in, and had hidden her in his closet when his parents entered the room. They found him out, castigated him, warned him never to bring her into their home again. He killed them both.

When adults become intimidated by the teenager and use him as a role model, he may become very frightened of his power and turn belligerent. He then unconsciously begs for controls. Many a promiscuous young girl has told her parents or a therapist, "I wanted to bring my sexual behavior to your attention so you would help me know what is right and what is wrong." She shows awareness of her lack of control and a wish for help with sexual feelings. Teenagers want to hear whether their sexuality should be repressed, or partially or perhaps fully expressed. They are never certain for long which course to follow.

In our contemporary scene adolescence is now more prolonged than ever. It is not unusual today for boys or girls in their late twenties to be dependent on parents economically, psychologically, and socially. There has also been a return of young married persons to their parental home, seeking to be nurtured once more. A recent popular book by Zenith Gross, *So You Thought It Was Over,* describes how hundreds of young people, many of whom are married college graduates, return home to live with their parents, who mistakenly thought their children had left to work out their own lives.

When adolescence is thus prolonged and dependency on the parents continues, the result is apt to be more resentment and power struggles between parents and offspring. Because of the prolongation of adolescence, the parental world often continues to be ambivalent toward the teenager.

We witness now, in the 1990s, more adolescent rebellion than ever. Sometimes the rebellion takes the form of the murder of outsiders. Far more teenagers are murdering unknown men, women and children on the streets, often holding them up for money to pay for the assassin's drug habit. At other times the rebellion consists of murderous wishes turned on the self. Teenage suicide has reached its highest level, increasing 250 percent in the last twenty years.

Though young people have greater sexual freedom than ever, they also face deeper sexual problems. In *The Age of Sensation,* an intensive study of four hundred college students not in psychotherapy, Dr. Herbert Hendin found that suicidal preoccupation was extremely high among young people. He also discovered that depression was common, the drug problem pervasive, impotence and frigidity frequent, homosexuality popular, and much enmity and great distrust between young men and women. Throughout Hendin's study, the typical college student seemed afraid to face his feelings. He seemed particularly threatened by sexuality that fused tenderness and eroticism.

A recent national survey of suburban teenagers concluded that drinking is more prevalent among high school seniors than among adults. Many experts believe alcohol has become a cornerstone of high school life.

As a seventeen-year-old student put it, "Everyone drinks. We drink to get drunk. It's fun." But she frowned in disapproval when crack was mentioned. Substance-abuse experts report that many teenagers appear to have embraced alcohol as the "one safe drug," that drinking is the result of parents terrified of crack.

The organization Students Against Driving Drunk, known as SADD, admits, according to one of its guidance counselors, that students drink a lot. The group has chapters in fifteen thousand high schools and four thousand junior high schools across the nation, thus acknowledging that drunk driving is an impressive reality.

To understand the consistent and intense rebelliousness of adolescents, we have to keep in mind much of it is related to their burgeoning sexuality. The intense desire for physical contact conjures up inevitable associations to earlier times when physical intimacy first began with the mother, father, grandparents and others, such as nurses, who might have been close.

Teenagers are inclined to be sadistic, because in experiencing sexual desires they often have to renounce the intense dependency wishes and yearnings to be nurtured that inevitably accompany early sexual desires. When teenagers feel uncomfortable with their sexual feelings but cannot acknowledge this, they may attack the person who attracts them. This is a temporary, albeit unnatural way to renounce sexual excitement.

The Presidential assassins who directly or indirectly confessed they were attracted sexually to the man they shot show us that violence may be connected to homosexual attraction. As children we all have a strong feeling that comprises both rage and sexual desire. If these do not become separated and modified as we grow up, they may act together in murderous violence.

While much of the rebellious and antisocial behavior of teenagers can be viewed as a way of warding off intolerable homosexual wishes, desires toward the opposite sex may also stir up anxieties. The great lovers of history were teenagers who turned their lovers into forbidden parental figures, one reason they shunned sex with the loved ones.

When a teenage girl unconsciously perceives her boyfriend as a father figure or an adolescent boy experiences his girlfriend as a mother figure, anxiety and guilt can impel them to be sadistic to supposedly loved partners. This result also occurs in some of the hostile, at times violent, even murderous attacks on teachers and other adult figures who conjure up in the teenager taboo sexual fantasies toward his parents. The teenager who rapes and hurts, perhaps even kills a teacher or older person, is clearly showing how forbidden he feels his sexual desire, as he believes he must go to the extreme in "hurting the one you love" even via murder.

Very often teenagers who run away from home or school are trying to escape sexually stimulating situations that make them feel helpless. Many an adolescent believes sexual wishes are tamed by changing the external environment. This hardly ever works and probably accounts for the reason why a large number of teenage runaways eventually return home.

When the teenager faces acute anxiety about sexual wishes that conflict with old taboos and stir up frightening dependency strivings, he feels even more helpless. Much teenage delinquency, teenage violence, and teenage murder is an attempt on the adolescent's part to ward off the intolerable conviction that he is weak and powerless.

He thinks that by taking action with a gun, fist, or rock, as the Central Park "wilding" gang did, he avoids the tension and pain that accompanies helplessness and powerlessness. For a short while, he believes he has proven how powerful he is.

The attempt to ward off feelings of weakness and powerlessness has much to do with what Erik Erikson points out is popular among teenagers—the assumption of a "negative identity." In the teenager's desire to defend against intolerable dependency wishes and in his resentment toward the adult world for not granting him the power and independence he craves, he often establishes a position of deep defiance and refuses to reason with anyone.

Teenagers often sensitize themselves to what the adults in their lives want, then do the opposite. Sons of football team coaches major in English literature, while offspring of devout Orthodox Jewish rabbis marry Catholics.

Negative identity is always a factor in teenage violence and murder. The teenager defiantly says to adults, "I will not submit to your rules and regulations, I will defy them. Only in this way do I feel powerful."

The runaway or the prostitute in many ways suffers from a negative identity. Such an adolescent is saying he will not cooperate with parents and adult society. On the contrary, he intends to do the opposite of what is sanctioned. By this defiance he enjoys the fantasied power of opposing a whole society. The fantasied power masks self-doubt and feelings of vulnerability. In all probability there is no self-confident, loving runaway or prostitute.

Another characteristic of the teenager is that he rebels against his increasingly strict conscience, one that will not allow him to feel human. As he becomes more sexually driven and wants to gratify more of the wishes that are consistently forbidden, he will feel greater guilt. The wish to masturbate frequently goes against taboos that have existed all his life. The desire to ravage a member of the opposite sex or even a member of the same sex also opposes strong taboos.

At the same time that the teenager wants more independence and the right to self-assertion, these wishes conflict with mandates to "Honor thy father and mother" and conform to societal sanctions. Because the teenager deeply desires much of what has been forbidden, he becomes guilt-ridden, sometimes unbearably so.

In contrast to guilt-ridden adults who can take their feelings to a forgiving parental figure, such as a therapist or minister, the teenager shuns help and direction from anyone. Some psychotherapists will not work with teenagers, feeling they are too volatile and rebellious.

Because the teenager feels guilty, he projects his guilt onto schools, churches, parents, and other symbols of authority. Instead of acknowledging how guilty he feels, he views his parents and other symbols of authority as inhibiting, criticizing, and threatening him. He attacks religion for being arbitrary, the school for being constricting, and his parents for being cruel.

Much teenage violence can be viewed as an attempt, albeit confused and self-destructive, to shut off the teenager's conscience. It is as if the teenager hears voices saying, "Don't have sex, behave yourself," yet does not recognize that the voices come from within the self. We might say most teenagers are a bit paranoid. And, like all paranoid persons, they do not accept their own guilty consciences but project them onto others.

A teenager is perhaps the most self-conscious person in our society. As he experiences new and at times uncomfortable sexual sensations, as he copes with intense sexual and aggressive fantasies that he may think are peculiar, even crazy, and as he tries to adapt to a new body image, he often projects his feelings of craziness, vulnerability, and peculiarity onto others. He feels "they are looking at me as if something is wrong with me."

He becomes deeply concerned about "being founded out" and thus most suspicious of those he believes are ready to criticize or mock him for feelings he himself considers forbidden. Because he is so ready to be pounced upon for what he personally cannot sanction, he is prone to pounce on others, to see them as the enemy.

Much teenage hatred exists because the teenager hates himself for wanting what he considers forbidden. But, like anyone else who feels guilty, he has the tendency to make someone else a symbol of his own conscience and attack that person. This takes place when teenagers attack teachers, policemen, and other symbols of authority.

As adolescence is prolonged and as mixed feelings in the external environment make it difficult to cope with teenagers, we see more and more teenagers indulge in alcoholism, drug abuse, and suicide. A recent survey showed that in New Jersey, a typical state, nine out of every ten high school students use alcohol and two thirds also use drugs.

Approximately one in twenty teenagers in the country is a drug addict. While taking drugs is an expression of many unresolved problems, it is frequently an attempt to surmount unacceptable, passive wishes, unpleasant feelings of vulnerability, and strong but unacceptable feelings of weakness.

While on a "high," the drug user can feel like a superman or wonderwoman omnipotently controlling the world. Many murders by teenagers occur when the adolescents are on a high, feeling like hostile Napoleons or belligerent Hitlers. Many murderous feelings occur when the young person is trying to get his needed "fix" and is frustrated. He then goes into a deep rage.

In understanding murder in the teenager we can appreciate why violence is prevalent. Any teenager, even those in fairly happy homes with two parents, will feel indecisive, ambivalent, powerless. Every teenager rebels somehow. Even those loved, appreciated, and nurtured will feel to a certain degree guilty, sexually inept, self-conscious.

If our most nurtured teenagers are rebels, it becomes clear why young boys who come from broken homes, who live in unsavory neighborhoods, who are members of a discriminated-against minority group, will feel murderous. If every adolescent is rebellious, regardless of how loving his formative years, it is apparent that a youngster who has been poorly nurtured, emotionally and physically, may emerge into a violent teenager. Perhaps even a murderer.

To what lengths does a civilized nation go to punish juveniles who commit murder? This question was discussed in the July 20, 1990, issue of *Psychiatric News,* a publication of the American Psychiatric Association (APA). A special article pointed out that with violent crime by juveniles on the rise in the last few decades, a country "torn by whether it should put any of its citizens to death for their crimes is being forced to face the dilemma of what it should do when those who have not yet reached adulthood commit murder."

The issue cannot be resolved without weighing considerations of law, psychiatry and morality, the article stated. The U.S. Supreme Court has given states the right to impose the death penalty and has refused to limit it to those who are at least eighteen. A Court majority decided it was cruel and unusual punishment to execute someone under fifteen.

Speakers at the 1990 annual meeting of the APA offered guidelines for deciding which juvenile murderers may benefit from psychiatric treatment, as well as opinions on whether minors should be eligible for execution and, if so, at what age. Few in medical or legal circles dispute the idea that the severity of the punishment meted out to juvenile murderers cannot be divorced from their development level. Dr. Elissa Benedek, an expert in forensic psychiatry and the current president of the Association, explained that the legal system has historically recognized adolescents' developmental immaturity through a separate juvenile court system that protects them from being fully accountable for their actions. She rejected capital punishment of any offenders as "abhorrent."

Benedek also said that psychiatric treatment for a substantial portion of juvenile murderers is often futile and not always an effective way to deal with this population. She described three groups of juvenile murderers, suggesting that two of them were candidates for psychiatric treatment—the 5 percent who are psychotic at the time of their crime and the 44 percent who, in the course of some other "interpersonal conflict," murder someone they know, such as a parent, sibling, or relative. These youngsters, most of whom kill with a gun, usually have been physically abused by the victim or linked in some crisis in which the killer sees no way out.

The third and largest group, about half of all juvenile killers, are those who commit an unplanned murder in conjunction with other crimes, such as rape, larceny or seeking money for drugs, often with one or more of their cohorts. Benedek described about two-thirds of them as high on alcohol or drugs at the time of the crime, and said that most of them killed with their hands or a weapon other than a gun. This last group would derive little benefit from psychiatric treatment, she said, and added that in this age of limited dollars and psychiatric manpower, treating them is probably a "waste of resources."

This particular societal problem—the very troubled teenager—is tied to chronic drug consumption and the rage of teenagers who live in inadequate housing and whose parents are usually separated. It will no doubt take years to solve.

PART 3

Murder in the Family

5

Murder of Children by Parents

"I'm going to give my children to Allah! Go, go, God's waiting for you," screamed Meenah Abdussalaam, as she pushed one of her children out the tenth floor window of her apartment building.

One day in October, 1989, a thirty-two-year-old woman whose home life had become desperately frustrating forced her five children into her clothes-strewn bedroom on the tenth floor of her apartment building in New York. She intended to kill them all, then to kill herself.

A fire truck had been returning from a false alarm. The firefighters saw a little girl, seven-year-old Zainab, dangling from the tenth floor, her fingers curled around the window guard. They stopped the truck and raced into the building just as a police car on patrol, driving by, also stopped.

Three officers dashed to the building and yelled to the child above them, "Don't jump! Don't jump!"

For a moment it looked as if the little girl was trying to obey them and crawl back in. As Fire Department Lieutenant John Lane later said, she lifted one leg up and was about to pull her body onto a ledge. But a woman's arm suddenly shot out of the window and pushed her downward.

Before the three police officers could reach the street

once again, Zainab had hit the ground. The firefighters rushed over with a resuscitator and tried to save her life.

A second child, three-year-old Hussein, was suddenly hurled downward. One of the police officers tried to catch the boy but he slipped through the officer's outstretched arms. The firefighters used the resuscitator on him as well.

At this point several of the firefighters had reached the tenth floor and broken open the locked door to the apartment from which the children had been hurled. They smashed through a heavy door the mother had blocked from the inside with furniture. Storming into the barricaded bedroom they found the mother preparing to force a third child, one-year-old Anna, toward a gap in the window guard.

The woman, identified as Meenah Abdussalaam, screamed, "I'm going to give my children to Allah! Go, go, God's waiting for you!" As she said this she pushed the little girl nearer the gap.

The firefighters grabbed the child in time, then tried to subdue the mother. She was, they reported later, "mumbling, 'Mohammed Elijah,' " as she repeatedly urged the children to jump. She told the men she was going to hurl herself out the window—she would be the last one.

The firefighters could not save Zainab, who died of internal injuries, fractures, and cardiac arrest. The boy was taken to a hospital in the neighborhood, listed in critical but stable condition. Two other children were identified as Askia, eight years old, and Fatima, four.

Officials reported that when one firefighter, John Gallagher, burst into the room Mrs. Abdussalaam hit him, cutting his lip.

Neighbors told reporters Mrs. Abdussalaam's world had broken apart, then collapsed a month before when she asked her husband to leave the family because of severe marital problems. She "kicked him out," said a neighbor, because "she was tired and could not handle it." The police reported she had received an eviction notice on the five-room apartment in which they lived.

Puzzled neighbors gathered outside the apartment building after the horrifying incident. Those who knew Mrs. Abdussalaam said there had been no indication she would commit an act as drastic as pushing her five children out the window. One neighbor commented, "She was the last one you would expect this of." They described her as a devout Muslim and pointed out that her children had the reputation of being polite, obedient, and "well mannered." She took them regularly to the nearby park, holding the youngest in her arms.

Over and over, when relatives and neighbors hear about someone they know committing murder, they quickly say, as they did about Mrs. Abdussalaam, that the person "was the last one you would expect to do that."

Why is this the typical response?

First of all, if a murderer is a relative or close friend, our immediate reaction is "This could be me." But who wants to acknowledge the murderer in all of us? Even someone who has spent several years on a psychoanalyst's couch and has been helped to gain the courage to face his most forbidden, terrifying impulses, will try to deny the murderer within. When we say someone close to us is "the last person in the world to have committed such a hideous act," we are protecting ourselves as we protest, "I am not a murderer!"

Many murderers spend months and years trying to deny their intense violent desires as they struggle to cope with the frustrations that stir up murderous wishes. Most of them, like Mrs. Abdussalaam, want to convince themselves and others that they are not on the brink of psychological disaster.

Many murderers are withdrawn, preoccupied with their inner thoughts. To most observers, they seem quite harmless. They live in their private world of depression, desperation, and wish for revenge on those who have hurt them as they try to protect themselves and others from murderous confrontations.

On October 25, 1989, shortly after Mrs. Abdussalaam's

desperate act, three other mothers in New York were charged with child abuse. In one instance, the child died.

Katrina Buchanan, twenty-two, of Brooklyn, was charged with second-degree murder after she allegedly stuffed a box of pepper into her two-year-old's mouth and he suffocated. The boy, Tyrrell, also showed signs of regular beatings. She had found him playing with the pepper and was furious at the mess he left. She then stuffed the box into the boy's mouth to teach him a lesson. Some of the pepper spilled out and the boy choked to death, police said. They rushed him to a local hospital where he died shortly afterward. A neighbor told police she had seen the child many times, "with black eyes and swollen jaw."

The second mother, who lived in the Bronx, a city emergency operator named Brenda Flood, thirty, was charged with abandoning her newborn baby in a vacant lot. He was found alive, wrapped in a clear plastic bag, after police received a tip on where he would be.

Also in the Bronx, Judith Zorros, thirty-six, was arrested when police found her six children half starved and crawling with lice in their apartment. One of the children, a ten-month-old baby girl, was treated for malnutrition at North Central Bronx Hospital.

All over the world many such mothers exist, mothers who kill or try to kill their children, unable to cope with bringing them up. After spending days and weeks, perhaps years, trying their best to figure a way out of their desperate, unbearable existence, they resort to murder. Mrs. Abdussalaam appeared harmless and had not hurt her children before, according to reports. She obviously suffered deeply, perhaps had been violently attacked by her husband, and did not know where she would get money to feed the children and herself. She probably also had been assaulted as a child by her mother or father or both, knowing violence well as she grew up.

The withdrawn, isolated person is more dangerous than the hostile individual who is able to verbally discharge what he feels and thinks. The anger and fear the withdrawn person has repressed may explode when he can bear no more of life. His constricted and unacknowledged rage underlies what neighbors and friends remember when they describe him as a "quiet, placid soul."

That children may cause stress and pressure in parents, resulting in parental violence, is far from an original finding. In the words of one of the most popular nursery rhymes,

> *There was an old woman who lived in a shoe.*
> *She had so many children she didn't know what to*
> * do.*
> *She gave them some broth without any bread,*
> *And whipped them all soundly, and put them to bed.*

This verse reminds us how long we have viewed children as stirring up the hatred of parents. The probable frequency of parental violence has been well documented, both in fact, as with Mrs. Abdussalaam, and in folklore, as with the old woman who lived in a shoe (whose husband is not mentioned and probably had little money, since dinner was only broth without bread, or may have deserted her).

One of the most unforgettable crimes ever committed against a child by a parent was the near death by burning alive of a six-year-old boy, David Rothenberg, in 1983. His father, Charles, took out his fury at his wife on his only child, going on a spree of "vengeful madness," as it was described in "The Reporters" on the Fox Network on February 11, 1989. Rothenberg was the son of a prostitute and had been raised in an orphanage. His childhood was one of severe emotional deprivation.

This television episode told how Rothenberg, who lived with his family in Brooklyn, had driven with David to Buena Park, California, ostensibly for a vacation and to see Disneyland. They stayed at the Travel Lodge in Anaheim. Following a telephone call to his wife, Marie, in Brooklyn, Charles decided to get vengeance. Marie was seeking a divorce and they fought over custody of their child.

He gave the boy sleeping pills, then carried out his death-trap plan. He had bought a can of kerosene and poured it all over David's bed. Then he lit a match and tossed it on the bed. As the flames burst forth, he ran from the room, closing the door. When other motel guests smelled the smoke and saw the flames from their windows, they raced to rescue the boy.

By the time firefighters arrived, over 90 percent of David's body was burned as he lay unconscious on the bed. What was left of him was "mutilated beyond description," as the reporter said. He was rushed to the local hospital, and doctors worked around the clock to save his life. During the following six years he underwent 150 skin grafts all over his body.

The father fled but was eventually caught and tried in California. He received what was then a maximum prison sentence of thirteen years for attempted murder and arson—conviction on the same charges today would bring a life term.

Officials at the prison in San Luis Obispo had no choice but to release Rothenberg on January 24, 1990. Meanwhile David's mother had met and married a detective working on the case, which meant she and David were living in California. David said, on the television program, that he was afraid his father would come after him, so he kept a BB gun by his bed. Police assured him they would keep his father far from him. For the next year Rothenberg had to live under the same roof as his parole officer and wear an electronic surveillance monitor at all times. He has been forbidden to enter Orange County, where his son lives with his stepfather, Richard Hafdahl.

The television program showed David today, riding a skateboard, able to move about, though his face somewhat resembles a gruesome mask. His voice, however, sounded natural as he answered the reporter's questions. Photographs of David before the burning show him to have been a very handsome boy.

The show also featured an interview with the father. He told the reporter, tears in his eyes, that he believed he should have received a life sentence, "even the death penalty," for such cruelty. He confessed he had intended to punish his wife by maiming their only child.

"I was very angry at Marie's mouth," he explained. "I know now I took it out on the wrong person. I just wanted to shut her mouth."

The reporter said frankly, "People out there think you're the biggest son of a bitch on two legs."

At this, Rothenberg broke down and cried openly. Then he said, as if speaking directly to his maimed son, "I love you. I will never remarry. I promise I will always be your father."

On the program David said he never wanted to see his natural father because he now had a father who loved him. The boy's fear is readily understood—it would be expecting the impossible for him ever again to trust his father.

What caused Rothenberg to attempt to murder his son? The father admitted he was driven by a murderous fury toward his wife that he could not control, for the derogatory names she called him and for seeking a divorce. Afraid to direct his rage at his wife, he chose a target far easier for him to manipulate, their son, knowing in this way he could wound her.

Anger this deep, culminating in the attempt to murder his son to get even with his wife, originated in Rothenberg's cruel childhood. We can only imagine his suffering when he lived for a while with his mother, a prostitute, never knew his father, and was brought up in an orphanage. His wrath at his wife undoubtedly echoed his fury at his mother for abandoning him, failing to love him, as his wife now threatened to do.

Fatal injury, not infectious disease, has become the leading cause of death among children in our country. Injuries, primarily from guns, have killed approximately ten thousand youngsters each year. Of these children, an alarming number are victims of homicide at the hands of their parents. This was reported in *Psychiatric News* on April 7, 1989. Children aged fourteen and under died from twenty-three types of fatal injury. The latter included not only death at the hands of a parent or the mother's lover, but drowning, motor vehicle and bicycle accidents, house fires, suffocation, poisoning, unintentional use of firearms, suicide, and homicide. Firearms are the most frequently used weapon.

Accidental injury—which, by the way, may often be not so "accidental" but unconsciously inflicted because of guilt either in the child or parent—contributes to "childhood morbidity and mortality," the researchers declared. They also stated that "nearly all the suicides" reported in the study occurred in the ten-to-fourteen age group.

Sociologists have shown that the likelihood of a parent abusing a child increases with the size of a family. Parents of two children have a rate of abuse 50 percent higher than parents who have one child to care for. The highest rate of abuse comes with five or more children. Although in many situations we say, "The more the merrier," when this applies to children it appears that "the fewer the happier." There are fewer shrieks, fewer demands, fewer responsibilities, fewer sibling squabbles, fewer decisions to make.

Furthermore, when children get together, the larger the size of the group, the more likely there will be fights. Sheer exhaustion can make many a parent feel quite vulnerable and, as we have said, the more vulnerable people feel, the more murderous they are likely to become. Our murderous feelings are a supposed shield against our vulnerabilities.

Thus large families often breed greater parental violence, and for centuries our society has provided parents with the right to use physical force—to strike, slap, and spank children believed to be obstreperous. Parents have been "beating the devil" out of children probably since Adam and Eve. Stories of being taken behind the woodshed and hit by a father's razor strop have been told for a long time. The early American colonists enacted "stubborn child" laws, which even gave parents the right to kill children they thought beyond their ability to control.

Our folklore, our fairy tales, our nursery rhymes, and our entire culture are full of reminders of the right of parents to use violence against children. Hansel and Gretel's mother and father abandoned their children to starvation in the forest when the parents ran out of money. The wicked queen told her huntsmen to take her young stepdaughter, Snow White, into the forest and cut out her heart because she was so beautiful—murder as the result of jealousy.

Despite several highly publicized cases of sexual abuse of children at day care centers, a study financed by the Federal Government and conducted by the New Hampshire Family Research Laboratory reported in 1989 that sexual abuse at day care centers, though still a serious problem, was less frequent than the abuse of children in their own homes.

The researchers estimated that for every ten thousand children enrolled at the centers, 5.5 percent were sexually abused each year. By contrast, they said that for every ten thousand preschool children, 8.9 percent were sexually abused in their homes each year, based on confirmed cases reported to the Government.

The $200,000 study, which took almost three years to complete, is the most comprehensive ever conducted on the subject. It examined substantiated cases of sexual abuse involving 1,639 children at 270 day care facilities across the country. The researchers looked at most of the reported cases that occurred from 1983 to 1985 in licensed facilities serving more than six children.

John Crewdson, a reporter for *The New York Times,* won a Pulitzer Prize in 1988 for his book on child abuse, *By Silence Betrayed.* Numerous television movies have focused on this topic, as well as books by or about multiple personalities, who usually had been sexually abused as children. Most multiple personalities are women, which seems to indicate that most sexual abuse is carried out on helpless little girls by their fathers or other masculine relatives, including grandfathers, uncles, and brothers.

Historians who have examined the history of child abuse, such as Lloyd De Mause, document centuries of violence and infanticide dating back to Biblical times. The advice "Spare the rod and spoil the child" was stated and illustrated many times in the Bible.

From ancient Rome to colonial America, children have been struck with rods, switches, and canes. They have been whipped, castrated, and destroyed by parents, often with the consent of political and religious institutions. Parents constantly rationalized their right to strike children, using Biblical quotations.

To "beat the devil" out of a child was a mandate to provide salvation for the child born corrupted by "original sin." De Mause and other historians have described the history of childhood as a "nightmare." The further back in history we go, the lower the level of child care and the more likely children were killed, abandoned, beaten, terrorized, and sexually abused.

How can we account for such brutality toward children for so many centuries? There are probably many reasons to explain such socially sanctioned violence. We will discuss two major ones and offer other possible reasons.

The first reason for parental violence is that children are supposed to exist largely, if not exclusively, to satisfy parental wishes. As many a parent will say, "I expect a child to give me pleasure and if he doesn't, I feel furious." While this notion might seem farfetched to the sophisticated 1990 man or woman, go to any Little League baseball game and watch parental violence as the mothers and fathers exploit their children so the parents can feel like winners. Many a 1990 father or mother later physically hits a youngster for striking out or missing a fly ball, or verbally attacks him.

The more a parent needs a child to bolster his self-esteem, the more the parent may be prone to violence. The more a parent has felt unloved, the more he will need the child to perform perfectly and love the parent consistently. As one battering mother put it, "I have never felt loved all my life. When the baby was born I thought he would love me. But when he cried, it meant he didn't love me, so I hit him." Because this mother remained such a child herself she could not empathize with her youngster—*she* needed all the caring.

The second major reason children have been abused for countless centuries is that the nature of childhood development has not been understood. Most adults, for eons, have assumed incorrectly that if a child is told to do something, he should do it at once. And if he is told not to do something, he should refrain from doing it.

It has only been late in the twentieth century that parents, teachers and others who live and work with children realize that children do not act from birth on like little adults but need much time and encouragement to slowly learn the demands of reality. They also need constant permission to make mistakes.

It is only recently that children are being regarded as children, not as little adults who live to gratify their parents' narcissism. It is also only recently that we have been able to consider the nature of physical and sexual abuse. While statistics show a high level of parental violence and sexual abuse of children, this disclosure may have appeared because violence is now seen for the first time as a serious social and family problem rather than an act sanctioned by society.

As long as a parent believes the child exists for his pleasure and that the child should know how to meet the parents' needs at once, parents will feel they possess the absolute right to hate their child and hurt him when the child does not make their lives happier.

Another reason children have been hated and treated so brutally over the centuries is that adults tend to condemn in children all behavior they cannot tolerate in themselves—what they believe sinful. When adults cannot accept their own yearnings for dependency, their own wishes to rebel against rules and regulations, their own sexual and aggressive fantasies, they are apt to be intolerant of children who constantly express these raw feelings and sensations.

Everything adults have felt evil in themselves they may project onto children. This is why children have been considered devils, tied up, swaddled, and tortured over the centuries. Adults believe children must be "restrained" and, in doing so, deny what they feel are their wicked wishes.

In the case of Mrs. Abdussalaam, we may conjecture that she could not tolerate her wishes to be taken care of like a child. Without a husband and beset by all kinds of new responsibilities, she no doubt felt like an overwhelmed child. By hurling her children out the window she may have been unconsciously throwing out the child within herself she could not tolerate.

We cannot underestimate how deeply the adult's internal feeling of sin and the devil become projected onto the child. As De Mause has pointed out, the number of ghost-like figures used to frighten children throughout history is legion. The regular use of hideous masks and devilish costumes for children is common at Halloween. In Germany, witches appeared in shops with stick brooms and a stiff brush at both ends. Children worldwide have been ordered to look at corpses, told, "That's what's going to happen to you if you don't behave." The unconscious wish of many a parent is to frighten the child to death.

The notion of empathizing with a child, acknowledging his right to loving nurturance, is a twentieth-century phenomenon. It was not until the mid-1940s that a psychiatrist, Dr. Margaret Ribble, in her book *The Rights of*

Infants, prescribed "tender love and care." She is the founder and inventor of "T.L.C."

It seems incredible that the Society for the Prevention of Cruelty to Animals was established before the Society for Prevention of Cruelty to Children. When New York church workers in the late nineteenth century tried to get help for a badly abused foster child, they found only the SPCA existed, so they founded the first chapter of a similar society for children.

If we keep in mind that the ideal child, until the twentieth century, was expected to take care of the parent, à la Dickens, then we understand why parental abuse has been so flagrant and pervasive. Furthermore, if for ages the parent was the "child" who had to be taken care of by a son or daughter, we realize why so many men and women who assume parental roles feel the right to psychologically and physically abuse their offspring.

The father-figure sergeant in the army or the marines feels an inalienable right to physically brutalize, even maim, those under him. It has been reported a number of times that a raw recruit in the military has been tortured to death. We know that those in parental roles may become violent murderers, such as workers in child care centers and mental institutions, wardens in prisons, union leaders, and high political figures who enjoy declaring war on other nations.

The killing of legitimate children was reduced slowly during the Middle Ages. Illegitimate children continued to be sacrificed regularly up until the nineteenth century. De Mause and other historians such as David Bakin, Samuel Radbill, and Eli Newberger have pointed out that infanticide during antiquity has usually been played down despite the fact that hundreds of clear references by ancient writers prove it was an accepted, everyday occurrence.

Although there were exceptions, the average child of wealthy parents spent his earliest years in the home of a wet nurse, then returned to his parents' home and to the care of servants. By age seven he was sent out to service, or apprenticeship, or school. The amount of time parents actually spent raising such a child was minimal.

Poor parents, who tended to have larger families, used many of the primitive forms of punishment described earlier, such as swaddling, violent spankings, and ghostlike figures to terrorize the child. Children were frequently sold or used as political hostages, as well as security for debts. Often they were tied to chains to prevent their crawling around the house, and until the late nineteenth century, strings were tied to their clothes to control them and to swing them about. If children were treated that way today, they would be called battered and abused.

Until the twentieth century the child often lived in an atmosphere of sexual abuse, which was often considered more normal than not. Boys who grew up in Greece and Rome were used sexually by older men as "boy brothels" flourished in many cities.

Because most adults found their own sexual impulses difficult to accept, children were beaten for masturbating, abused physically for their sexual curiosity, and castigated if discovered in sex play. More often than not, when a child was sexually abused by an adult, the latter rationalized that it was a form of punishment. Even today children are struck angrily by parents and teachers who derive erotic and sadistic pleasure from the act, although they insist, "We're just giving deserved punishment."

A more subtle kind of murder occurs, one that does not destroy the child immediately but causes what we could call slow death over the years.

Fathers who sexually seduce their little daughters fall into this class of semimurderers. It is estimated that more than 50 percent of the women in this country are survivors of child sexual abuse at the hands of fathers, older brothers, uncles, or grandfathers. Today, because of the increase in divorces, the stepfather has become part of the incest scene.

This was graphically portrayed during the *Geraldo* television program on October 27, 1989, titled "Daddy Dearest." One father, behind a screen, told of the feelings of disgust he'd had when he raped his daughter. A daughter who appeared on the program told how her father raped her at the age of nine, and she'd been pregnant three times because of his subsequent rapes. It is estimated that at least ten thousand pregnancies yearly have resulted from incestuous rapes.

The father behind the screen also told Geraldo that he first raped his ten-year-old daughter when his wife left him, taking three of the children. Geraldo asked if he used his daughter to fill the nurturing wife and mother role. The father agreed he had molested her to make up for the emotional gap his wife left.

"Didn't your conscience bother you?" Geraldo asked.

"No," the father said. "My daughter did not complain. I thought she wanted it." Then he admitted, "She had a trust in me which I violated. She figured I knew best. I was the father."

"How did you get caught?" Geraldo asked.

"My oldest daughter, who was living with us, said something to a neighbor about Donna sleeping with me every night and the neighbor called the authorities."

At first both he and his daughter denied to the police that incest was involved. But eventually she broke down and admitted it. He confessed after he learned she would have to stand trial in front of a jury and he did not want her to go through this. He admitted they had sex three times a week over a four-year period. He received a jail sentence of nine months.

Another young woman on the program said she was seduced between the ages of ten and fifteen by her alcoholic father. She finally told him, "I'll kill you if you don't stop." She said she blamed herself and felt responsible for the act of incest.

The audience applauded when Geraldo said, "Even if you stood naked in front of your father, begging him to have sex with you, he was still the adult and should have known better."

Another woman, who said her father raped her at two and then again at ten for five years, sometimes "putting objects inside me," described how she "lived through nightmares every night and still do," and added, "There's not enough a father can say that will ever make it right."

She went on, "I couldn't understand how this wonderful man I loved could hurt me so. He held his hand over my mouth so I wouldn't scream." She also said she felt a child had to obey the parent, could not say no, because "we were taught to do what our parents told us to do."

The audience was warned during the program that if a child feels "dirty or defective," is frequently ill or depressed, a chronic overeater, afraid to disrobe before anyone, or acts in aggressive or violent ways, these are possible clues to parental rape.

Perhaps one of the most serious realities in parent-child relationships is that many parents still hate children with as much intensity and display almost as much violence in the early 1990s as they did in ancient Greece and Rome.

The Greek or Roman father held absolute power over his child's life, including the right to kill the child. This is not so different from the practice today in which parents possess the right to put a child in jail if he disobeys, or to subject him to the controls of the Persons in Need of Supervision (PINS) program. Similarly, children or their representatives who feel vengeful toward parents have the right to seek Termination of Parental Rights (TIP) orders.

Although today's parent-child relationships are more influenced by modern psychology, there is still a tendency to view children who misbehave, who do not conform, who are deeply troubled, as "bad" children descended from "bad seed," who must be treated punitively so their "badness" will be blasted out of them.

That the amount of hatred and violence in parents toward children is rampant seems evident in the very existence of the popular and active organization called the International Study of Organizations Persecuting Children, which has its own newsletter. Also, a national bestseller of 1990, *Toxic Parents* by Dr. Susan Forward, would not have drawn such a large audience unless daughters and sons felt injured by their emotionally disturbed parents.

Both the violence in our culture and our awareness of it are increasing. It is important to reiterate that violence is most acute between parents and children in poor families. Parents act most violently, become more murderous, in economically deprived families where opportunities are limited, deprivation is intense, and scarcity of resources frequently generates extreme competition between family members, often culminating in violent acts such as murder.

While we find that a number of middle- and upper-middle-class parents abuse their children, social scientists agree that the higher the family income, the more the likelihood of affection and warm feelings between parents and child. Obviously it is easier for the parent under less financial strain to concentrate more on the emotional needs of his child.

Yet in any statistical account of parental violence or murder, the poor or minority family will be reported first. The more affluent parents can often keep their violent behavior a secret. Thus we cannot conclude violence is absent in affluent families. It is just seldom revealed publicly. Hateful feelings of parents toward children and children toward parents may also be expressed less directly than in poorer families.

It is also conceivable that hatred may at times be more intense in families where there is no physical violence than where physical violence is used to cope with frustration. Many psychotherapists have worked with affluent families whose members hate each other intensely but may not express the hatred openly. In any discussion of violence we have to keep in mind that violent behavior may express such feelings as emotional neglect, sarcastic derision, or the scapegoating of a son or daughter.

To enjoy being a parent and to be able to love a child, the parent as a child had to be enjoyed and loved by his mother and father. The angry parent is an adult who cannot understand, respect, and guide not only his own child but the unhappy child within himself.

A parent becomes most violent when his child's behavior triggers conflicts and vulnerabilities that reflect he parent's own conflicts and vulnerabilities. If the parent, as a baby or young child, was left to cry, not given the tender loving care needed during infancy and childhood, on hearing his own child cry he may throw a temper tantrum or scream at the child. He may even, as in some cases, kill the child, as Joel Steinberg did. We do not know what little Lisa said or did—perhaps no more than look at Steinberg in a way that reminded him of his own forbidden sadness or anger or hopelessness—but it provoked enough of a horrendous memory for him to murder her. A parent will hate his child for reviving in him buried emotions of fear and rage stemming from the time he was deprived of attention he needed desperately from a parent.

Many an infant has been murdered or abandoned when the parent, usually the mother (but sometimes the father or a live-in boyfriend of the mother's), is so needy she cannot feel empathy for her infant's pleas for help. Some mothers have placed their baby on a stranger's doorstep, or mutilated or killed him. The mother abandons her child the way she once felt abandoned and *still feels abandoned*. She tortures the child in the manner she formerly felt tortured and *still feels tortured*.

An emotionally depleted mother put her newborn daughter under a parked car in a midtown Manhattan alley on October 31, 1989, leaving the infant to die from exposure to the cold or by getting run over. Fortunately, Ruth Pearl, a nurse at nearby Roosevelt Hospital, and Paul Evans, a former policeman who happened to be in that area, heard the baby's cries and rescued her.

Police believe the baby was born in the lot nearby. Pearl was going home from a double shift when she passed Evans. He asked, "Did you hear a baby cry?" It was so dark at first they could not see the baby and returned a second time to make sure they had not missed it. They found the seven-pound-one-ounce little girl, with placenta and umbilical cord still attached, naked under the parked car, her head placed against the front wheel. Pearl ran to Roosevelt Hospital to call a paramedic, who came and wrapped the baby in a blanket, then took her to the hospital. She was treated for mild hypothermia and reported in good condition.

Both Pearl and Evans visited the infant. Evans brought some baby clothes and told hospital authorities he and his wife were thinking of adopting her. If the weather had been a true October cold, she might not have lived but nature provided a day in the sixties. Combined with the concern of a nurse and a former policeman, that probably saved her life.

Some parents do not care what happens to a newborn baby. They feel they must get rid of it. They cannot cope with being forced to become a caring adult—they resent the loss of their freedom deeply. These parents were never allowed the pleasure of childhood; they were forced to take care of themselves when they needed soothing, embracing, holding, and other forms of physical and emotional comfort from a nurturing adult. Often, when a child deprived of these necessary pleasures becomes a parent, he will try to get rid of the unwelcome addition to his household, not caring whether the newborn lives or dies.

There are also parents who try to cope with the new child by seeking suffocating closeness. The parent wishes to compensate for the lack of emotional contact he felt as a child from his parents. But such a parent may withdraw early expressions of his yearning to be close and become punitive when the child attempts to separate from him. This parent relives the feeling during his childhood when he felt abandoned by parents. As his own child asserts independence, the parent feels neglected, falls into a rage.

When parents have not received reasonable and loving

discipline as children, they become very angry if their child refuses to accept their authority. One mother wrote Ann Landers: "Last night I did something that really frightened me. I was helping our son with his homework and he refused to try to solve the math problem. He just kept saying 'I can't get it. I can't get it.' I became so infuriated I started to slap his face as hard as I could. I couldn't stop. Today the little guy had black and blue marks on his cheeks. I was so ashamed I didn't let him go to school."

This mother in all probability was a child who always had to produce—for parents, teachers, grandparents. To *not* produce the right answers, as her son did, meant she deserved to be beaten. She gave her son what her parents and others felt she deserved—severe physical punishment.

The child driven to conform, driven to know the right answers all the time and swiftly, often holds back an anger he cannot express directly, but which is always ready to emerge. Many an obedient child, inhibited and constricted throughout his childhood and adolescence, on becoming a parent feels consciously for the first time his pent-up rage and wish to kill. He does not realize that this murderous feeling reflects what he originally felt toward his restrictive parents. He now displaces it onto his child as he says in effect, "You must conform the way I had to. You will receive what I received—a slap in the face and maybe worse—if you don't conform."

Before a parent can respond to a child with love, warmth, and appropriate discipline when needed, he has to resolve his own hatred toward his parents, a hatred aroused when he was very young and unable to express it because he feared the giants who controlled his life. If he cannot face this early hatred, his own child becomes the recipient of the slings and arrows of his early "outrageous fortune."

Although we live in an age of sexual enlightenment, many parents of the 1990s still find it difficult to cope with a child's burgeoning sexuality. If a parent was not helped during his childhood to accept his sexual fantasies and wishes as normal, he will become punitive toward the child who shows sexual curiosity or becomes involved in sex play.

One mother severely spanked her four-year-old son for getting undressed in the company of a four-year-old girl playmate. The mother later told her therapist, "I was never permitted to play like that—it's disgusting and evil." The therapist, over time, tried to show a more benign attitude than the woman's parents had. He helped her be more accepting of her own sexuality so she could then accept her son's sexuality with more equanimity.

Many parents cannot tolerate their sexual fantasies toward a child, feelings only recently recognized as universal. It is important to accept that all parents will have sexual fantasies toward their children. It is impossible to bathe, dress, and undress a child without being somewhat aroused in fantasy.

When we cannot tolerate the feeling of being sexually attracted to someone, adult or child, one way of coping with our discomfort is to remove ourselves from the person who attracts us. This happens to the father who feels uncomfortable with his feelings toward his teenage daughter and withdraws from her. Or the mother who feels frightened of her sexual fantasies toward her handsome teenage son. Parents of both sexes may be uncomfortable with their fantasies toward children of both sexes.

Withdrawal is one way of handling the discomfort, hitting and beating is another. Both methods stir up rage in the child and may make him a potential murderer who will act in the same way toward his child. Rare is the killer who has not been raised in an extremely hostile atmosphere set by a parent or parents. He does not have to see murder committed in his family, it is enough if he just sees violence expressed. A child will try to outdo a parent in whatever hostile acts he sees the parent express as the child grows up.

Parents who sexually abuse a child, or adults who seduce a child, indulge in what we have called "soul murder." This is murder of the psyche, murder of the spirit of the child, murder of the child's spontaneous sexuality. Such early seduction by a parent halts the child's natural emotional and physical development. For the rest of his life the child may paralyze his sexual drive and become celibate, feeling deep guilt. Or he may be promiscuous with members of the same or opposite sex.

Some parents will kill an adolescent daughter or son if they feel the child has been sexually "untrue" to them. They are acutely jealous of the child's attachment to someone else. James Hyames, fifty-nine, fatally shot his eighteen-year-old daughter, Lisa, then barricaded himself inside his home in Mastic, Long Island, and held off the police for seven hours before killing himself.

The dead girl's stepsister said, "He told me he shot Lisa because she was in bed with a boy." He evidently spared the boy. As he told the stepsister, "I shot Lisa in the back and she's lying in a pool of blood. I think she's dead. The whole floor is full of blood." He added, "I'm fine." And then, "I'm going to kill myself because I don't want to go to prison."

His wife, Mycine, had run out of their home at noon and called the police moments before Lisa was shot. When they arrived, Hyames fired at them. The officers retreated, to ask for hostage negotiators. Two hours later, the father fired again, this time grazing an officer's head. Finally he turned the gun on himself at seven P.M.

His wife told police, "I'm not surprised. He's been a hurt man for years. You could never put his heart back together again." She was saying he had suffered as a child and inflicted his suffering on the daughter he felt betrayed him sexually. (As a little boy, he may have felt his mother had betrayed him sexually with his father, perhaps with other men, too.)

Sometimes sexual abuse comes from a foster parent and involves a child of the same sex. Over the last decade a Bronx man offered shelter to ten abandoned boys and had been sexually abusing four of them. Robert Gonzalez, forty, unmarried, had legally adopted or become a foster father to physically and emotionally troubled children. Authorities believed he offered the only stable home many had known.

But according to police, his ten-room house in the Hunts Point section of the Bronx was little more than a prison where their "father" sexually abused them. A police officer told reporters, "The strange part is, these kids love him still. He's the only person who ever took care of them." The youngest of the four boys he was accused of abusing was five years old.

Gonzalez's abuse apparently went undetected by city adoption officials because he had a clean police record and seemed genuinely to care about the boys, many of whom were described as "unadoptable." Neighbors said the children were "loud and disruptive," and that Gonzalez's mother, who also lived in the house, practiced a West African voodoo-like religion.

While much overt sexual abuse is brought to our attention by the media, a great deal of abuse, both covert and subtle, is never discussed. This includes parents parading in the nude and overstimulating their children, and parents and children sleeping in the same bed, which creates excessive sexual excitement and anxiety in the child. There is also seductive conversation which stirs up the child and leads him to feel sexually aroused and uncomfortable.

All these subtle, covert acts of seduction are a form of abuse in that they create anxiety and stir up hatred in the child—hatred of the parent and the self because of anxiety and guilt. While the female child is the one usually discussed as the victim and the male adult as the perpetrator, it is now known that the number of boys who are sexually victimized by both females and males is not insignificant.

Is sexual abuse of children more prevalent in the 1980s and '90s than earlier? *Nursery Crimes,* a recent book by David Finkelhor, Linda Meyer Williams, and Nanci Burns, dealing with sexual abuse in day-care centers, dramatically points to the many adults who sexually abuse young children. The authors cite the 1984 arrest in California of Virginia McMartin and six of her employees for the alleged abuse of 125 children over a ten-year period at McMartin's day-care center. After the longest trial in Los Angeles history, all charges were dropped. A few months later another highly publicized case in Minnesota resulted in indictments against 24 parents and other adults for sexually abusing more than fifty children.

Though sexual abuse of children may not be more prevalent now than it has been for countless centuries, its widespread documentation is being accepted as a "given" for the first time in our society.

Childhood sexual abuse, which at times reaches violent and murderous expression, exists because of the many adults in our society who have severe sexual problems. It has only been in the last fifteen or twenty years that sex therapy is acknowledged as a legitimate form of therapy, not because adults have recently acquired sexual problems but because we are now, as a society, more ready to acknowledge this, rather than to continue to pretend it does not exist.

In the 1990s many adults who sexually abuse children are admitting they are too frightened to take part in adult sexuality. Sexually abusing adults were usually physically and psychologically abused children. They never learned to love because they were not loved but rejected for their sexual feelings, which never matured beyond those of a frightened child.

We will discuss violence and murder in marriage in Chapter 7, but it is important to point out here that when marital partners cannot love and enjoy each other sexually, they are more prone to be seductive and sexual—or sexually abuse—with their children.

If their feelings of vulnerability become more intense and the inevitable hatred of a spouse soars to the surface, one way of expressing this hatred is to attack the child instead. We saw this earlier in the case of Charles

Rothenberg, who tried to kill his son by setting his body on fire because he was furious at his wife for planning to divorce him.

Immature parents are often very jealous of their partner's relationship to the child. One way of expressing the hatred that always accompanies jealousy is to hurt, maim, or even destroy the child. This not only repeats how the murderous parent felt as a child in his violent home but shows the displaced fury aroused by his spouse.

Problems connected with parental care have been given serious consideration only in the present century. Before then, it was assumed the child was either a good or bad seed. The notion that parents play a central role in how their children develop emotionally was almost ignored before the advent of modern psychology.

Ideally, the parent should be able to love his child, be of assistance in allowing the child to mature, help the child break free of parental ties as he grows up and learns to control his own life. But psychotherapists and researchers in child development have shown that widespread conflicts still exist in all these areas.

Only when parents have known love as children do they possess the inner security to give comfort and affection to their children. If parents were hated as children, they will hate their children. If the parents' childhoods were marked by neglect and violence, they will become neglectful and violent parents. They will misuse and abuse their child because they still remain children who, emotionally speaking, have not broken free of their tormenting parents.

It is a sad commentary on our civilization that although we have made strides in many areas, such as science, technology, and communications, we have not significantly surpassed our forefathers in reducing the hatred parents show toward their own children.

6

Murder of Parents by Children

"Children want to be individuals and we make them a tiny entity among millions. They want a modicum of safety; we present them with the spectacle of a frightening world. They seek adventure and we don't provide it except for the crudest murder and war toys."
—*Frederic Wertham,* A Sign for Cain

A twenty-three-year-old graduate psychology student in Chicago, who we shall call David Gold, was the son of a psychologist and a nurse. His older sister, Sally, twenty-five, was a resident physician in a Chicago hospital.

David was described by his psychologist father as a "lovable child," and this description was echoed by David's mother. He "always did what he was supposed to do," they boasted. His mother proudly explained, "David never cried when I weaned him. And he always listened to me and to his father. He never questioned our authority."

At school, in the 1960s, David was considered the "teacher's pet." He listened carefully to instructions and always carried them out. He was considered a good sport, cooperative with everyone in and out of school. He was never known to disagree with anyone. Repeatedly his teachers said, "David Gold always is considerate of others. He puts the wishes of people of all ages before his own."

At college David became a highly successful psychology major and graduated cum laude. Just as he had related to his sister with concern and consideration, David seemed to attend to the needs of his girlfriends and boyfriends. His peers, parents, family, relatives, and teachers all felt he was an affable, cooperative, gentle young man.

He attended his sister Sally's wedding, serving as best man. In characteristic fashion, he was considerate of and cooperative with all who were present. Three weeks later, to the shock of everyone who knew him, twenty-three-year-old David bought a gun, went home, and shot and killed his father. Then he shot and killed his mother. Finally, he shot and killed himself.

A note was found where the murders and suicide took place, in his parents' bedroom. The note read, "I've been trying too hard." He could no longer put up with the pretense—he had been concealing a Mr. Hyde for all those years.

Why does a young man from a well-to-do family, in which both parents were described by those who knew them as loving and caring, murder them? How do we account for the fact that David, who had always obeyed the commandment "Honor thy father and mother," suddenly decided to violate another commandment, "Thou shalt not kill"? Why did such a conforming, obedient, cooperative young man suddenly turn into a violent, destructive son who destroyed his father, mother, and himself?

Although we cannot be certain of all David's motives, perhaps a major clue can be found in his childhood. To feel loved as a child, David was compelled to submit to the iron will of his parents, even though their treatment of him was not in accord with the wisest and most humane way to bring up a child.

Obedience, discipline, and conformity were impressed upon—forced upon—David probably from the day of birth. He was led to conclude that as long as he did "the right thing," he would be loved. To oppose his mother and father, to dare show anger, was an unforgivable sin in his mind.

David's story teaches us that some submission to parental authority, and authority in general, is necessary in any family or social order. But if it is carried too far or if it seems a rigid adaptation to adult commands, its effects can be very damaging to the growing child. When the submissive child acquiesces to parental wishes as consistently and as rigidly as David was forced to do, he develops within himself a deep, lasting hatred for his compulsive parents. The hatred, the wish to defy, is defended against throughout childhood and adolescence. But somehow, someday, it is bound to erupt and cause catastrophe.

Perhaps it was more than a coincidence that David killed his mother, father, and himself three weeks after his sister Sally's wedding. Possibly he viewed her happiness as a feeling denied him throughout his life. He may have felt he was always forced to conform while Sally was loved for being herself, loved without rigid rules.

Perhaps too, as David thought about Sally's marrying and enjoying the always available sexual pleasure marriage brings, as well as the love of a partner, his deep jealousy emerged—jealousy he had buried all his life along, doubtless, with his sexual yearnings for her when he was a little boy. And perhaps his parents, especially his mother, made him feel that any expression of sexuality as a little boy was forbidden. While we will never be sure of the causes of David's extremely violent behavior, we can be fairly certain that for twenty-three years he behaved like a machine operating properly for its owners—his mother and father.

When any human being is forced to act mechanically, to bury his sexual and aggressive feelings, he will feel misunderstood, taken advantage of, lonely, acutely vulnerable, and intensely murderous. Unless someone like David is offered an opportunity to face, understand, and discharge his murderous feelings, he is apt to become a candidate for murder or suicide.

Another such case, on March 22, 1989, involved a sixteen-year-old boy, Brian Britton. Wearing Army fatigues and calling himself "Rambo," Brian slaughtered his forty-four-year-old father, forty-two-year-old mother, and eight-year-old brother, Jason, on a predawn rampage with a shotgun in his rural home in Poughkeepsie, New York. His eighteen-year-old sister, Sherry, was shot in the head and chest but miraculously survived.

After pumping the eight shots into his family—in a scene that lasted less than three minutes—Brian hid the shotgun in the attic, jumped out his second-story bedroom window, and ran next door to the home of his uncle, Richard Britton. Brian reported that his father was shooting the family and Britton called the police.

The carnage, which started shortly after 5 A.M., followed a running battle over Brian's school attendance, according to Poughkeepsie Police Chief Stanley Still, who described Brian as possessing a "Rambo fixation." After he was arrested, police found his bedroom covered with memorabilia from the blockbuster *Rambo* movie series, as well as military paraphernalia, including a smoke grenade and canvas ammunition packs. He confessed his crimes to the police and was placed under a suicide watch in the Dutchess County Jail.

Brian's schoolmates were not surprised that he was arrested for shooting his family. Several described him as an "obnoxious loner" who always wore Army fatigues and was obsessed with everything military. One girl said he would pretend to be shooting at classmates, "he'd point his fingers like a gun and go 'Got you' or 'You're dead, you creep.' " A neighbor recalled Brian "had a knife with him at all times, a big Rambo knife." The neighbor's daughter, his cousin, informed police that Brian's younger brother Jason, whom he killed, told her that Brian would at times "cut himself and watched the blood run."

Violent crimes committed by children increased 22 percent in 1989 over 1988, with rape up 14 percent, it was announced on the TV program "The Reporters" on September 2, 1989. "We're going to see more psychopaths than ever before in the history of America, some as young as eight or nine, a lost generation of kids who appear to have no conscience," one reporter remarked.

He continued, "Thousands have begun a lifetime of crime. They come from broken families, parents who abuse them, as they now abuse others." He warned, "The violent kids of today become the hard-core criminals of tomorrow." He said they all "suffered devastating traumas in their early life."

According to counselors, psychologists, and social workers at a conference in Keystone, Colorado, in the fall of 1989, thousands of young Americans "sexually abuse thousands of even younger Americans every year. Thirteen-year-old rapists are not uncommon nor are eight-year-old victims."

The National Center for Juvenile Justice reported that for thirteen- and fourteen-year-olds, the arrest rate for rape has more than doubled since 1976 and the arrest rate for lesser categories of sexual assault is up 80 percent. Young boys as well as girls are common victims. Girls are at highest risk in their own homes, usually from family members, while boys are at highest risk outside the house, often from someone they know and trust. Boys tend to feel freer and more spontaneous than girls, and seek to prove their machismo, allowing outsiders to exploit them.

Sexual abuse, experts say, is a particularly contagious form of violence in that most sex offenders have been victimized as children. They felt they had no allies, no one to whom they could turn for help. A recent study found that nationwide treatment programs for sexually abused children have grown by more than 66 percent since 1986.

The negative consequences of conformity in our society have long been recognized. Eric Fromm in *Escape from Freedom* points out that many people are afraid to be independent because they have been so pressured to conform as children. David Riesman in *Individualism Reconsidered* and *The Lonely Crowd* talks of the "other-directed" person, referring to the man or woman who fears the consequences of nonconformity and remains compliant most of the time. William Whyte in *The Organization Man* describes the emotional disadvantages of an excessive reliance on authority. In *The Meaning of Love in Human Experience,* Reuben Fine speaks of the "good" child who is fundamentally "not so good" in that he feels guilt-ridden, far from emotionally happy or healthy.

Invariably, conforming children have parents who, like David Gold's mother and father, also appear very conforming on the surface. But when we look at the emotional makeup of such parents, we find they are riddled by doubts, torn by unconscious resentments, and deeply unsure of themselves in many important areas of living.

Often such parents respond to their children only when the latter act like little slaves. The parents are grossly insensitive to the child's fears, hopes, fantasies, and, above all, resentments. They rarely feel it is legitimate for a child to express, let alone discuss, angry feelings, particularly anger toward the parents. Incidentally, those who have more potential for murder than the average person often seem to have had a family life in which a great deal of conformity was required. Controlling parents constantly offer advice or disapproval, set up obstacles every time a child or adolescent wants to show autonomy.

Over and over we hear that the child who has killed his mother or father invariably sees his parent as a very restrictive person who demanded obedience, as well as being obsessive in his expectations. Many researchers point out that often the girl or boy who murders a parent has felt enormous pressure to conform, endured great restrictiveness and deprivation of pleasure, as well as a harshness emanating particularly from the mother. All these obsessive qualities are not acknowledged by the child until adolescence or later.

The child is usually afraid to show any sign of rage. He suppresses it most of the time, keeps trying harder and harder to conform. Like David Gold, after adolescence a vast amount of rage may erupt, followed by the murder of a parent or sibling.

As we understand how the child who must obey the parent's every word or be subjected to harsh discipline often may become a murderer, we also see, as in the case of David Gold, why such a murder upsets most of us—because the child in us has been striving valiantly to be an archconformist and most of us identify with the "good" part of the child.

Many were shocked to learn that an eighteen-year-old girl in Hartford, Connecticut, Karin Aparo, convinced her twenty-one-year-old boyfriend, Dennis Coleman, to strangle her forty-seven-year-old mother to death with a pair of pantyhose in her condominium on August 5, 1989. Karin's lawyer filed notice of an "insanity" defense and said he would present expert testimony relating to "a mental disease or defect." A psychiatrist and a psychologist who examined Karin described her as mentally ill, attributing her illness to years of abuse by her mother. Teachers, friends, and relatives of Karin attested to this. Coleman pleaded guilty to murder and conspiracy to commit murder.

Many children who kill a parent have been forced into a premature and rigid obedience. They are reported as quiet and well behaved, but behind the scenes there often stands a father who, after he has been murdered, is described as demanding that family life center on him—the family must eat, sleep, watch television according to his mandates. Should anyone rebel, the culprit is severely punished. Often the father is alcoholic and prone to temper tantrums, and he frequently intimidates his family, who endure their lives in "quiet desperation," as they try to believe that "Father knows best."

When a child is pressured to conform, forced to submit to unfair parental dictates, he begins to feel a strong defiance within. He wishes to fight back, but these rebellious wishes and the courage to carry them out do not emerge until adolescence or later, when he feels more of an equal to his punitive parent.

* * *

All adolescents tend to defy their elders at times, for this is vital to becoming independent of early caretakers, part of maturing. But defiance of elders by young people has increased greatly in the last two or three decades. Fighting, taking drugs, selling drugs, indiscriminate sex, dropping out of school—these appear quite common. Adults are much less certain of their authority, as seen notably in families but also in schools and colleges.

More and more we see brutal violence by younger and younger age groups. The police look for children and adolescents as perpetrators in murder cases whereas formerly they would not even have considered them. The present-day significance of the famous Leopold-Loeb case in Chicago is that, while in the 1930s, it was virtually unheard of for an eighteen-year-old boy to commit murder, in contemporary America murder by youths has become almost commonplace. The juvenile gang springs up in many communities and its violent acts are frequent, carried out by younger and younger children, often ferocious and brutal.

The "ferocity of youth violence is up," a school official announced in *The New York Times* on November 11, 1989. The story revealed that Victor Herbert, executive director of the Division of High Schools at the Board of Education, had met with principals and teachers and warned them that "the level of potential violence" among young people "is higher than I've ever seen it before."

Herbert said he was concerned about a rash of recent incidents, including the murder of eight high school students in little more than a week. He also mentioned rampages where groups of teenagers assaulted or robbed pedestrians on the East and West Sides of Manhattan and in Rego Park, Queens.

These incidents, he said, reflect "reckless abandon" and "carelessness" that permit many youngsters to discard inhibitions that traditionally constrained adolescent behavior. Today's teenagers take the attitude, "I'll knock you over if you get in my way."

"I don't want to be a Cassandra," Herbert stated, "I don't want to be frightening people. But it is more dangerous for riders on the streets and subways than it has ever been before in my limited memory." He added, "In general terms of young people responding to adults, there doesn't seem to be any of the fear, any of the sense of the old-world values like respect."

The ingredients that have contributed to this "caldron of violence" are "racial strains and discrimination, a growing gulf between those who have and those who have not, parents too busy to pay attention to their child's behavior, the polarization produced by the 1989 mayoral election, the violence in 'rap' and other popular music," he said. He warned that the growth of crack, weapons, and gangs have rendered that mixture "explosive."

With reference to rap music, B. Adler points out in her introduction to *Rap: Portraits and Lyrics of a Generation of Black Rockers* (St. Martin's Press) that "rap—the great rock 'n' roll of its day—is rich with all the qualities that have always made rock 'n' roll great: big beats, sex, wit, humor, nonsense, adolescent rebelliousness, grown-up revolutionary sloganeering, wild haircuts, cool clothes, and more sex. And, like all of the greatest rock 'n' roll, it opens up the possibility of escape: escape from dreary middle-class convention and deadly underclass desperation alike."

She adds that "just as rock 'n' roll sparked the integration of America ten years before the establishment of the Civil Rights acts of 1964 and 1965, rap, via 'Yo! MTV' is beginning to bring the races together in the Nineties. . . . It is impossible to miss the excitement of the real thing, and young white kids have taken to rap in direct proportion to their exposure to it."

One of the songs in the book, from *Children's Story* (1988), with lyrics by R. Walters, concludes with the words:

> *He was only seventeen, in a madman's dream*
> *The cops shot the kid. I still hear him scream.*

> *This ain't funny, so don't you dare laugh*
> *Just another case about the wrong path*
> *Straight and narrow, or your soul gets cast.*
> *Good night!*

Another song, "Planet Rock," concludes:

> *Love, life, live*
> *Come play the game, our world is free*
> *Just do what you want, but scream!*

Returning to Victor Herbert's warning about the high level of potential violence among young people, he admitted there was a "racial component" to the violence but stated it was not exclusive to any one race. He pointed out that black youths were involved in attacks in Central Park and the West Side but young whites took part in the killing of a black teenager in the Bensonhurst section of Brooklyn in the summer of 1989.

"I struggle to keep it in a racial perspective," he said. "I don't want to feed into the hands of those who see it as a minority problem. It is. Minorities hurt each other more than anyone else. But it is everywhere."

Poverty is not the only cause, because there have always been poor neighborhoods and they did not yield the kind of violence that has existed in recent months, Herbert pointed out. Significantly different these days, he added, is that the violence is often purposeless, the victims unknown to their attackers. The stakes have also risen sharply, with youths more willing to hurt others and themselves to get money for illegal drugs not only to feel out of this world but to dress better and buy fancy cars.

Directly below this interview, the *Times* carried the headline "2 Boys Are Stabbed at a School in Brooklyn." It described how there had been a clash the day before between two groups of teenagers in the cafeteria of Intermediate School 117 in the Bedford-Stuyvesant section of Brooklyn. Two wounded students, fourteen and fifteen years old, were taken to the hospital. The fourteen-year-old was charged with assault and possession of a weapon.

Vandalism has reached an all-time high. In New York City alone it costs the schools millions of dollars a year. Teachers in many other cities are vulnerable to attack and murder as knives and improvised weapons are frequently used on them. Almost every day in New York a teacher is beaten by a pupil. In five school days there may be twenty assaults against teachers.

The change in the direction of greater violence has been high among girls too. A taxi driver was held up one day as two boys and two girls, all in their teens, entered his cab. They threatened the driver, took all his money, and one girl hit him over the head with her shoe, breaking his glasses.

There is also an increase in acts of sexual violence in youths. Many young persons discharge murderous feelings through rape and other sexually violent practices, as noted in Chapter 4 when the jogger in Central Park was raped and almost murdered.

Numerous reasons are offered to try to explain the increase in violence among children and teenagers all through our nation, particularly the increase in murders of parents by offspring. Dr. Frederic Wertham, in *A Sign for Cain*, an exploration of human violence, offered his opinion concerning the increase in violence among young people:

> They want to be individuals and we make them a tiny entity among millions. They want a modicum of safety; we present them with the spectacle of a frightening world. They want to learn; we put them in overcrowded classes in school. They seek adventure and we don't provide it except for the crudest murder and war toys. They wish for amusement and we give them unrewarding—but for us remunerative—stereotyped comic books and screen fare. The adolescents want to confide their health worries but

we have dismissed the family doctor and offer them advertisements and commercials of phony patent remedies, and so on.

Writers and social commentators note the increased divorce rate and its impact on making children and adolescents angrier. The breakdown in the solidarity of the American family is frequently cited in books and newspapers. The lack of stable values is another reason for more violence on the run. The proliferation of the drug culture, as noted, often leads to more murderous behavior, as does the tremendous increase in alcoholism among youth.

While all these factors have had a deleterious influence, we would like to suggest another that has not often been noted and which may account for the increase in murderous feelings of children toward parents and parental figures. Just as children centuries ago were turned over to a wet nurse, only to become furious and murderous because they felt abandoned and lonely without a parent, in contemporary America a quite similar process is occurring.

The age in which a child is sent to nursery school or to a day-care center becomes earlier and earlier. The nature of our society is such that infants and toddlers do not obtain the consistent, tender loving care they desperately need early in life. During the last three decades more and more children have not received consistent nurturing by even one parent. More and more children are turned over to strangers who care for them in groups such as the day-care center or the pre-nursery school. Baby-sitting in many ways has taken the place of parenting.

If we study the rage in young people that has been mounting and mounting, we see that many of them have been forced to conform and adapt prematurely to rules and regulations of the nursery or day-care center when they were too young and emotionally too fragile to do so.

Like David Gold, who also went to pre-nursery school and was nurtured in groups rather than on a one-to-one basis early in life, many children feel abandoned, then enraged because they are asked to take care of themselves rather than being taken care of.

It is important to emphasize that all children, particularly during the first three years of life, need constant and consistent one-to-one attention by a parent. Today, many under the age of three have to adapt to a group too early.

We also see a phenomenon known as the "latchkey child." Millions of children go home after school to a house that holds nobody. Like David Gold, when their parents appear, the children act cooperative and conforming, too terrified to reveal, even to themselves, how furious and unloved they feel.

The child who feels loved and attended to, particularly during the first three years of life, does not become a murderer. Our society does not recognize how much it induces rage in children when it forces them to become prematurely independent, prematurely adapt themselves to groups, and insist that they prematurely obey, when they need the freedom to think and to play spontaneously.

Another insufficiently recognized factor in promoting the violence of children and teenagers is the way in which parents and other important adults in the child's social orbit subtly encourage violent behavior. Child psychologists have noted that children prone to become delinquents and to act out other forms of antisocial behavior, including murder, are subtly reinforced in their violent behavior by parents as they witness parental violence in the home. Some children see their own violence condoned by parents; others are treated violently by a parent.

A minister consulted a child therapist because his adolescent son had been caught stealing cars and the minister felt ashamed and embarrassed. He also felt deeply guilt-ridden, as though *he* had stolen the cars. As he became more involved in the family counseling that ensued, he slowly realized how much excitement and secret pleasure he derived from his son's escapades. Unconsciously, he had encouraged his son to steal, to act like the boy he had wished to be. Without realizing it, he aided and abetted the crime. Many parents encourage their children, particularly teenage sons and daughters, to rebel in ways they had wanted to as children but felt too inhibited. We have to understand this in looking at children's murderous behavior.

The perfectly normal infant is, by definition, "egocentric, greedy, dirty, violent in temper, destructive, profoundly sexual, aggrandizing in attitude and without much of a conscience." He is also "opportunistic, inconsiderate, domineering and sadistic."

This description, by the famed British psychoanalyst Dr. Edward Glover, closely resembles that of a murderer. We may describe the murderer's mind as that of a child who has never grown up. He has been forced to regress to a childlike state of mind and behavior but, unlike the child, now possesses the adult strength to kill someone he hates.

Such murderers, whether children, teenagers, or adults, have never been helped by parents to emotionally mature. They want what they want at the moment they want it, like a baby, and turn into a killer when they do not get it. They feel like the baby and small child felt—"Death to the one who frustrates me"—only now they have the power to act on their wish.

If we can accept the fact that the normal baby is, for all practical purposes, by adult standards a murderer and a criminal, then we start to understand even more clearly why people murder. We recognize that the murderer has never been helped to mature emotionally, remains a "baby murderer." His life has become so tormenting that he must regress to the "baby-murderer" state. All of us carry the child within us through life; all of us return at times to an infantile state and can be considered potential murderers.

To understand more clearly the child who murders a parent, we should try to understand the reasons why the child was not helped to grow up emotionally, why he never felt an inner certainty or trust in another person. When the bond that exists between child and parent is chiefly one of fear and hatred on the one hand and an inexplicable loyalty and yearning for love on the other, as appeared in David Gold, the child cannot free himself of the emotional bond without explosive violence.

We know now that when a child is not accepted as having sexual feelings, when the sexual dimension of life is considered taboo, the child reacts with fury. When boys are not helped to be boys or appreciated as boys, and girls are not helped to be girls or appreciated as girls, their potential for violence is vastly increased. We know too that if a parent wanted his first child to be a boy but it turns out a girl, he will unconsciously get across the message that he wished for a boy and treat the girl as a boy. Or if a parent wanted a girl and a boy is born, that message, too, will come through to the child as he grows up.

One phenomenon observed among children and teenagers who are violent or commit murder may come as a surprise. Often, many feel deeply guilt-ridden. How do we account for the fact that a murderer, a so-called psychopath or sociopath, has this overdeveloped conscience?

When a child must conform to rigid rules and regulations, when he does not feel loved most of the time, when he feels he must be more an automaton than a spontaneous child, he feels a burning fury. Most children as they grow up cannot permit themselves to acknowledge this because if they were to do so, they would face abandonment, retaliation, or the withholding of love.

When children feel this initial rage at being unloved and unappreciated, they wonder what they have done wrong—they look within themselves for the cause of this mistreatment. Unfortunately, children who have known only foster parents their whole life will inevitably feel inferior to children with parents. The abandoned child always believes something is wrong with him and this is the reason his parents did not want him. It is difficult for him to feel as secure as the child with parents, even the child with cruel parents. This was true of Charles Manson and of Willie James Bosket, Jr., neither of whom ever knew his father. It is also true of Marilyn Monroe, who committed suicide at thirty-six. She never knew her father, barely knew her mother, and lived with a foster family the first eight years of her life. She was then returned to her mother, then back to foster families in five months when her mother went insane.

The angrier a child feels toward his mother and father, the more he becomes ashamed of himself and the greater the guilt. Rather than hate the parent on whom he is dependent, he hates himself. Rather than accuse his parent of neglect and wrongdoing, he accuses himself of failing to be a good child. He tries to conform more and more, be an obedient child, repress and suppress all hatred.

Whenever such a child derives even the smallest amount of happiness, he will feel guilty. He thinks, How come I feel pleasure and no one is yelling at me? He feels he is getting away with something. He says to himself, "I'm getting away with murder," and feels one up on the world for the moment, before his guilt again takes over.

Freud, in a brilliant essay, "The Criminal out of a Sense of Guilt," describes the person who feels very guilty even when he derives only a modicum of pleasure, believing he should be punished instead to diminish his sense of guilt. Unconsciously he may commit an act that provokes punishment and lands him in jail. If his guilty conscience is not eased in prison, when freed he is unconsciously driven to do something "bad" once more so he can return to prison and lessen temporarily the voice of is punitive conscience.

Many murderers are so guilt-ridden, so deeply tormented by punitive internal voices that they kill not primarily to get rid of another person but to get rid of the torture of their guilt. They know they will either be incarcerated for life or given the electric chair and this removes to some degree their oppressive guilt.

One man, because of such guilt, confessed to a murder he had committed nine years before. Richard Degrijze, thirty-seven years old, walked into the Forest Hills police station in Queens, New York, on November 9, 1989. He told police he did not know her name but he had killed a woman in 1980. He was not sure of where she lived.

Detective Joseph Bianco, who had worked on the squad during that time, asked Degrijze a few questions, then pulled out the case folder on Jacqueline Hogan. This thirty-eight-year-old bank employee had been fatally stabbed twice in the chest when she resisted robbery outside her apartment in Forest Hills in August 1980.

Degrijze described to the detectives details of the slaying that only the killer could have known. It was a case in which there had been no suspects and the knife had never been recovered. Degrijze was now married, had a family, and recently lost his job at a warehouse. It was then he decided to confess because of the guilt he had carried with him over the years. He was charged with second-degree murder, attempted robbery, and weapons possession.

One of our Presidents showed deep guilt and the need to be punished when he attained the highest office in the land. He acted in a far less murderous way than most, yet one that brought punishment. When President Nixon could no longer tolerate the pleasure of a successful presidency, he unconsciously arranged to be thrown out of office. He may have felt guilty about surpassing a dead brother and becoming superior to a father known to have a violent temper, according to Robert Morris, in his book *Richard Milhous Nixon*.

Morris describes how Frank Nixon once whipped his oldest son, Harold, so hard that the boy's screaming could be heard throughout the neighborhood, and "angrily" yanked his three sons from a stream where they were wading, then tossed them back in, yelling, "If you want water I'll give you enough," as their aunt screamed, "Frank, you'll kill them, you'll kill them!"

Richard Nixon later wrote of his father, "It was his temper that impressed me most as a small child." Nixon's mother, Hannah, according to Morris, acknowledged that her husband "would not hesitate using the strap or the rod on the boys when they did wrong." She said that after her husband died she felt deeply about his "shouting at the boys," adding that she tried not to scream at her children because "it does something to a child." It frightens him and because of his fear he will then feel an anger he must bury.

Both the young and the old who feel emotionally troubled often utter disguised cries for help. They suffer intense hatred, then feel guilty but cannot resolve their tortured feelings. This painful quandary is exemplified in the life of baseball player Joe Pepitone, once a star Yankee first baseman.

Joe was known to have endured a tempestuous relationship with his father. They appeared to quarrel day in and day out. It was alleged that during one argument Joe said to his father, "Drop dead!" and in fact his father did die soon thereafter. It is likely that for the rest of his life Joe will feel he murdered his father with his impulsive words. That is what a child believes.

From then on, this extremely capable athlete unconsciously arranged to get thrown out of baseball games by umpires and admonished by coaches and managers. He was eventually ostracized by the baseball profession, accused of peddling drugs. In all probability he felt like a guilty son who warranted punishment for wishing his father dead during one angry moment.

When a child holds this death wish for a parent, he feels as though he *is* a killer, as stated earlier. And if he feels like a killer he needs to be punished. And if he needs to be punished, he cannot enjoy anything for long. If he dares enjoy himself, he believes he is getting away with murder and must be caught.

One way a person who believes he is a murderer at heart can seek punishment is to commit murder. Often the guilt-ridden murderer keeps performing violent acts until he is caught. The killer with the interesting nickname "Son of Sam" was such a young man, adopted and living in a home where, like Kallinger, he never felt loved. He shot couples in cars parked in dark spots where they kissed and enjoyed sexual intercourse.

His foster parents had allowed him to sleep in their bedroom for the first years of his life and no doubt he saw them in intercourse many times. A number of killers have mentioned such a situation in their youth. Both his sexual feelings and his guilt at having them, as well as his rage at his parents for stimulating the feelings, must have been monumental as he transferred onto the young couples in the cars the fury he felt in childhood at being so tantalized.

When a policeman finally trapped him, he said with much relief, "I am the Son of Sam. Here I am."

Another murderer made a direct plea to the police to catch him. On December 10, 1945, in Chicago, William Heirens killed thirty-year-old Frances Brown, a secretary in the Chicago office of a business machine company after three years of war service as a Wave. He wrote on her beige living room wall the words:

> For heavens
> Sake catch me
> Before I kill more
> I cannot control myself.

Less than a month later, on January 6, he choked to death Suzanne Degnan, a six-year-old girl sleeping on the ground floor of her parents' home in North Chicago, and left a note asking for $20,000 in bills. He disposed of her body by cutting it into pieces and depositing them in various sewers. But he left his fingerprints on the note. That June his fingerprints were taken when he was caught trying to rob an apartment. After checking about seven thousand sets of prints against those on the Degnan note, a fingerprint expert in the police Bureau of Identification found that Heirens's fingerprints in the robbery matched the ones on the Degnan note. He was tried and convicted of murder. He had in a way helped the police catch him through the fingerprints.

* * *

In any discussion of a child murdering his parent, it is important to point out that *no* son or daughter is exempt from murderous feelings. As they grow up, all children possess fantasies of violence toward their parents. All children, in their dreams at night and in their daydreams, plan and plot ways to send their parents to their graves. It is only a matter of degree, as we emphasize throughout this book, between the child who commits murder and the child who wishes to murder but does not act on the wish.

When we can accept the fact that all sons and daughters want to murder their parents and thus each of us is a murderer at heart, we will be much more understanding of and empathic toward the one who actually murders his parents. He is not all that different from everyone else except that his early life has been more tormenting and more traumatic. Therefore, he has limited frustration tolerance and less self-control.

Why do the minds of all children, all adolescents, and all adults occasionally whirl with murderous fantasies toward parents? Let us consider several reasons.

First, every one of us from the cradle to the grave longs for an omnipotent, omniscient parent. Nobody, at any age, wishes to go it alone through life. We each want to feel supported, we all look for someone who is wiser, stronger, and cleverer than we are. Since no parent can fulfill the role of the all-wise, all-clever, all-perfect soul, no parent is ever exempt from his children's hatred to some degree.

Even the most rational person in the world retains the childlike fantasy that his parents could be perfect if only they wished to be. Many adults—perhaps most adults, maybe all adults—even after their parents are dead, cling to angry thoughts toward the mother and father and in effect ask, "Why didn't you love me more? Why were you so inconsiderate? Why didn't you show more sensitivity? Why were you so hateful at times I needed your support?"

These questions, which everyone on earth hurls at his parents, whether it is a poor child in Iran beaten unmercifully by his father or a wealthy child in a Manhattan penthouse who has never been touched in wrath, show that all of us nourish the fantasy that our parents could have been more loving and move giving if they had only wished to be. The more childish we remain, the more we believe our parents possessed the love to give but held it back. Thus we go on thinking and thus the more murderous we feel toward them.

Sons and daughters have other reasons for wishing to arrange for their parents' prompt dispatch. During the process of growing up, a child is frustrated many times by parents for one reason or another. Every child is weaned from the breast or the bottle and resents this very early deprivation. Every child is bombarded with many do's and don'ts, hating each instruction. No child—for that matter no adult—welcomes restrictions. To a lesser or greater degree, we all hate it when our pleasure is curbed.

No child likes being kept out of the parental bedroom and every child hates the privileges and pleasures his parents or older siblings enjoy but which are forbidden to him. No one who has been frustrated in the process of growing up can eliminate all of his hatred toward those who have said "no," disciplined him, at times perhaps struck him.

Thus, revengeful feelings toward our mother and father are normal in the course of emotional maturation. When we add to this the fact that every parent in the world has to deal with his own emotional immaturities, insensitivities, anger, then it becomes even clearer that hatred of parents is a universal phenomenon.

The murderous feelings toward our parents carry with them the creation of guilt in all of us. Many of the major psychological problems, such as depression, alcoholism, masochism, work failures, addictions of all kinds, are really expressions of the deeply buried guilt we try to cope with all through life because of murderous wishes toward our mother and father.

Alexander Portnoy, in Philip Roth's classic novel

Portnoy's Complaint, recalling "that extended period of rage that goes by the name of 'my adolescence,' " says, "What terrified me most about my father was not the violence I expected him momentarily to unleash upon·me but the violence I wished every night at the dinner table to commit upon his ignorant, barbaric carcass. . . . And what was especially terrifying about the murderous wish was this: If I tried, chances were I'd succeed."

Portnoy also recalled, as he ran from his half-eaten dinner and slammed out the door, his mother warning, "Alex, keep this back talk up . . . continue with this disrespect . . . and you will give that man a heart attack."

One of the least accepted human reactions is the burdensome guilt that follows murderous wishes. The son or daughter who seizes a gun and shoots his or her parents suffers deep guilt. Most of us have received some love from our parents and therefore cannot feel murderous without wishing to punish ourselves.

Guilt always follows aggressive acts because everyone who is aggressive past the age of two, which means most of us, has learned that aggression is taboo. Every criminal, every murderer, every violent person, no matter who he is, feels he should be punished. Even Hitler felt he had to be punished by his girlfriend, as he asked her to whip him.

Judith Viorst in her bestseller *Necessary Losses* points out that many if not most sons and daughters, in the course of growing up, fear they will give their parents a heart attack even when they do not show disrespect but merely wish to leave home and be on their own. "Indeed, it has been proposed that asserting our right to a separate existence can unconsciously feel as if we are killing our parents and that, therefore, most—maybe all—of us have some degree of separation guilt," she said.

One woman of forty-six told her therapist, "I remember with fear at my daring to tell my mother, when she asked me to live with her after my father got a divorce and married another woman, 'Mother, I couldn't. It would result in matricide.' " Her mother asked what that word meant and, after hesitating a moment, the daughter explained, "the murder of a mother by a son or daughter."

This woman confessed to the therapist, "And when my mother died twenty years later in a home for the aged, I felt I had killed her because I was too selfish to live with her and make her life happier."

The therapist explained, "You wanted to see yourself as very powerful—perhaps omnipotent—as if only you could take care of your mother." The woman eventually discovered a new way to look at the relationship between herself and her mother. Instead of feeling like a weak, guilt-ridden daughter who needed to be punished, she began to realize grandiose wishes had distorted her thinking. She had in no way been responsible for her mother's death.

Some psychologists and psychiatrists have even viewed growing up as a form of homicide. As Dr. Hans Loewald, a psychoanalyst, once said, "The assumption of responsibility for one's own life and its conduct is in psychic reality tantamount to the murder of parents."

Loewald, like other psychoanalysts, takes the point of view that severing emotional ties with parents seems like killing parents. Many adults tend to view their emotional emancipation as killing something vital in their parents—as if they were contributing to their parents' deaths, the way the woman described above had felt.

It is very difficult, even for the experts, to understand the difference between wishes and reality, between wanting to murder and actually carrying out the wish. As a result, many murderous thoughts and acts are misunderstood or not understood at all. To emancipate himself from parents and protect his independence, to strive for autonomy, a child might fantasize saying to a parent, "Drop dead!" but there is a tremendous difference between wishing a mother or father would disappear forever and actually killing the parent.

Parents who feel unsupported, misunderstood, rarely appreciated, may say to the child, "You are hurting me, you are killing me!" Sons and daughters may then believe they are murderous culprits because they have not been able to differentiate their wish from the deed. One mother would shriek at her eleven-year-old son whenever he disobeyed her, "You'll be the death of me!" He grew up terrified he would be held responsible some day for his mother's death.

Let us not forget that fantasies of violence and death wishes exist in every one of us. All sons, all daughters make themselves victims of great guilt. They become frightened of their hostile wishes because of what therapists call "magical thinking," the first kind of thinking a small child is capable of. It precedes our being able to reason, to realize the wish is *not* the same as the deed, that we cannot control events with our mind. Our thoughts cannot kill, no matter how strong they seem.

Viorst gives an example of how a daughter's murderous thoughts assumed magical proportions as the daughter felt she had killed her mother. "I know a smart, sane woman who had gone through a terrible time with her mother," Viorst says. "Bitter and angry, quarreling with her every day, she fantasied one evening, as she drove there for a visit, that her mother had suffered a fatal heart attack. Arriving at the street, she saw an ambulance roar past, stopping with a screech at her mother's front door, and paralyzed with fear she watched a team of medics rushing in with a stretcher and out again with the body of the woman who lived upstairs from her mother."

The woman told Viorst, "I was utterly convinced when I saw that ambulance, that I had given a heart attack to my mother. And I have to confess that part of me still believes in some nutty way that my magic missed and got that poor lady instead."

Viorst's vignette poignantly demonstrates how much all of us want to be magical and omnipotent. We would like to press a button and immediately achieve our deepest wishes. As we want our mother or father dead, we believe we can somehow arrange this and live in peace.

None of us fully outgrow our magical thinking because

none of us want to accept how truly powerless we are in influencing not only other people but some of the pernicious ways of the world. Some feel so powerless they must kill to gain a modicum of strength. One reason we all have the wish to kill is because it is so difficult to accept our vulnerabilities, weaknesses, and imperfections. We become so upset with our limitations that we want to commit murder on anyone who frustrates us. We believe we can influence the fate of our parents, siblings, and all others who stand in our way.

There is one reason it is important to discuss the universal wish of sons and daughters to kill their parents. This phenomenon, more than any other, explains why most people cannot enjoy the success they are capable of achieving and enjoying. The main reason men and women, children and adults, cannot savor success or, in some cases, dare not even aspire to it, is their deep guilt over murderous fantasies toward parents. Millions of us could seek and be more comfortable with success were we not so overburdened with guilt. We could take pleasure in making more money, being more creative, enjoying sex more, treasuring relationships with others.

Why does the thought of success cause such crippling guilt? Because success, when we cannot truly enjoy it, makes us feel we have "made a killing." When we cannot feel proud of ourselves in work and play, even though we are successful, we are indulging in magical thinking. We still believe our murderous wishes toward our parents, siblings, or others are at work despite our achievements and that we must suffer for achieving by denying the right to success. Often the guilt is subtly expressed through "accidents" that harm various parts of the body or symptoms of bodily ailments and other self-destructive acts.

Much of the hatred children show toward siblings in many ways is another form of murderous rage toward parents. All children believe that if their parents really loved them, they would not have produced another child.

Freud pointed out, "A small child does not necessarily

love his brothers and sisters, often he obviously does not. . . . He hates them as his competitors and it is a familiar fact that this attitude often persists for long years until maturity is reached or even later without interruption."

Just as we deny our murderous fantasies toward parents, we also tend to deny them in ourselves and in our children. Children are supposed to be their "brother's keeper." But all children feel murderous toward brothers and sisters because every child believes his siblings are more loved than he is. The nature of the human mind is such that each of us wants all the attention every moment of the day. Thus, every child with siblings to some extent feels ignored and wishes to kill his brothers and sisters, whether they precede or follow him.

This is expressed by the child who greets the newborn baby by asking his mother, "You mean he's staying?" or "When are you going to take him back to the hospital?" Or who accidentally on purpose drops a cup of hot soup on the new brother's or sister's face. Anna Freud includes among the normal characteristics of early childhood "extreme jealousy and competitiveness and impulses to kill rivals."

All of us want to kill off siblings and all of us at times want to kill parents. Just as parents tell their children "the facts of life," another fact of life can be provided by parents who wish to be helpful to their children. This is the fact that murderous feelings toward parents and siblings are universal and such feelings should be understood and accepted as natural, rather than repressed as evil. The child should verbalize these feelings, rather than condemn them and bury them in the unconscious part of his mind where they become even more terrifying and produce great guilt.

If more children were given the opportunity to talk about their murderous feelings and fantasies, particularly toward a parent and a sibling, we would have many fewer murderers.

7

Murder in Love
and Marriage

"Marriage is a wonderful institution—provided you like to live in an institution."

—*Groucho Marx*

It was Alfred, Lord Tennyson who said, "Marriages are made in Heaven." That was in 1864. According to our divorce rate more than half the marriages made today in this country were made in hell.

Many wives have left husbands and even more husbands have left wives twenty to thirty years after marriage. One daughter remembers her father falling in love with his secretary, who was thirteen years younger than her mother, and after eight years leaving his family to marry her. Whereupon the daughter's mother turned to her and said angrily, "I'd like to kill that woman!" The daughter, then twelve, said, shocked, "You can't mean that, Mother!" Her mother replied, in a softer tone, "I hope this never happens to you but if it does, you'll know why I feel like murdering her."

Many a married man conducts an affair with his secretary because romance in the office seems exciting, far removed from the routine existence at home. As a rule he plans only to have a temporary affair, preserving his relationship with his wife. But if he decides to divorce his wife and marry his secretary, soon after his remarriage he may start to feel guilty and murderous toward his secretary, blaming her for breaking up his home.

A thirty-five-year-old obstetrician divorced his wife of ten years to marry a twenty-year-old secretary. Two years later the secretary consulted a psychologist. In her first session she broke down and sobbed. Then she explained, "For three years I worked as secretary for my husband when he was married to his former wife. Then they got a divorce after he told her about me."

There was indignation in her voice as she went on, "Would you believe that within three months after we married he started to treat me like dirt? Swore at me. Insisted I was now just like his wife, that I had lost all the charm I had before we married."

When it is the wife who walks out on the husband, he may not only threaten to kill her but actually do so. On March 16, 1989, Joseph Pikul was convicted of bludgeoning and strangling his second wife, Diane, forty-four, who left him after taunting him for being a transvestite. It took a jury in Goshen, New York, nine and a half hours to find the fifty-four-year-old man guilty of second-degree murder. He had killed her at their weekend home in the Hamptons, on Long Island, wrapped her body in a tarpaulin, and dumped it miles away beside the New York State Thruway in Newburgh on the Hudson River. In cases like this, the husband is always a strong suspect.

One of the most gruesome murders of the year 1986 was that of Rita Fioretti, who lived on City Island, New York, with her husband, Robert Fioretti, a Bronx policeman, and their two children. He reported she had disappeared, supposedly into thin air. Police eventually suspected he had murdered her but could not prove it. Somehow, it always *seems* incredible to the general public that a policeman, hired to protect us, will kill a wife or other innocent person.

One month after his wife's mysterious disappearance, Fioretti married his pregnant radio car partner, Officer

Maureen Brooks, and she moved into his City Island home with her two daughters by a previous marriage.

Police searched endlessly for Rita Fioretti's body but could find no trace. Then in April 1988, parts of a woman's body, including her headless torso, were found floating in the East River. They were identified as belonging to Rita Fioretti. There was not enough proof, however, to charge Fioretti with her murder. But a year later, in March 1989, he was charged with sexually molesting the two young daughters of his second wife. In November 1989, he was indicted and dismissed from the police force for illegally forging his wife's signature and transferring $17,616 from her account to his after she vanished.

Reports of Fioretti's child abuse first surfaced when officials at his thirteen-year-old stepdaughter's school on City Island noticed bruises on her body. She and her eleven-year-old sister told authorities that her stepfather fondled them and also beat the younger children in the family, Rita's five-year-old son and Fioretti's two-year-old daughter by Maureen. The four youngest children were placed in foster homes after the allegations were made.

As of this writing, Fioretti was to appear at the Bronx Federal Court on October 24, 1990, on the charge of sexually abusing several of his children.

Occasionally, it is the wife who murders her husband or arranges for the killing. In the state of Washington one battered wife, thirty-seven years old, ended what she called seventeen years of terror and abuse by hiring a gunman to kill her husband. Identified in *The New York Times* of October 29, 1989, only as Ms. Alanize, she was granted clemency and freed from prison by Governor Booth Gardner. He said that he believed she and her four children had suffered enough and society would not be threatened by her release.

The clemency order was the Governor's first in five years in office. At the time she faced trial, Ms. Alanize faced the fact that the battered woman syndrome could be used as a defense only if the defendant had killed the abuser in self-defense in an actual or imminent attack. Prompted by her case the Washington State legislature passed a law allowing lighter sentences for abusers' victims who strike back.

According to Barbara Laskin on "The Reporters," March 31, 1989, half the women in this country are physically abused each year by the men in their lives. Most of them are battered wives. Only a small number leave their sadistic husbands. About 15 percent are murdered, like Rita Fioretti.

Between 1982 and 1987, it was reported that 6,083 women were killed in their homes by husbands. Phil Donahue said during a program discussing battered wives on June 21, 1989, "The most dangerous place for a woman in our society is her own home."

Laskin deplored the ineffectiveness of the restraining orders of our courts on violent husbands. Many of them murdered their wives while defying court orders, such as Adam Berwid, who had been sent to Pilgrim State Hospital on Long Island, after brutal assaults on his wife. Mrs. Berwid was in the throes of divorcing him to marry another man, who would then act as father to their children. One summer day a psychiatrist at the mental hospital granted Berwid permission to leave for a few hours. He took the train to the house where his wife lived with their two children, stole into the cellar. Then he swiftly ran up the steps and into the kitchen, where he slashed his wife to death with a knife as she ran toward the telephone to call the police.

When Berwid was caught, the psychiatrist treating him was duly reprimanded because he failed to realize how mentally disturbed his patient was. Berwid was then sent to a state prison's mental hospital on the orders of a court judge.

On June 1, 1989, an eighteen-year search ended for one of the nation's most wanted fugitives, John E. List, a Westfield, New Jersey, man who vanished when his mother, wife, and three children were found shot to death in 1971. The case had appeared on a May 21 segment of "America's Most Wanted," a Fox Network program.

Federal Bureau agents in twenty-three offices had hunted across the country, then into Europe and South America, before ending up in Richmond, Virginia, with the arrest of a man calling himself Richard P. Clark. Authorities revealed that the suspect, a college-educated, churchgoing accountant, was John List. He had changed his name but kept his profession, and had married a woman who knew nothing of his past. He was careful to avoid any trouble with the law that might expose his fingerprints.

The television program had showed a sculptor's bust of what List probably looked like after eighteen years, including a telltale scar behind one ear. A viewer of the program called the police. List, now sixty-three years old, was positively identified by his fingerprints. The arrest stunned his wife and the affluent New Jersey community.

The New York Times ran a full account of his capture on June 2, 1989, along with a large photograph of his first wife, Helen, his daughter, Patricia, and his two sons, John Jr. and Frederick, all attractive facially. The former Westfield, New Jersey, chief of police, James F. Moran, had carried List's file over the years and doggedly followed leads, even after retiring in 1986. He told reporter Robert D. McFadden, who wrote the *Times* story, "How can a guy murder five people and walk away? That has bothered me for many years."

List seems to have been a very depressed man who held back murderous fantasies all his life, trying to deny them. Anyone who constantly denies that he feels murderous sooner or later may discover that he can no longer control his feelings. List had to deny his hatred and rage until he could no longer contain it. It got the better of him, like a rushing stream of water that breaks the dam.

Though poorer men are in the majority when it comes to killing their wives, murderous husbands come from all socioeconomic classes. They kill to get revenge when a wife threatens to leave them. Or to get even for past hurts, real and imagined. Or for falling in love with another man. Or for reminding them of a mother in childhood who was brutal.

Wives also kill or pay hit men to murder their husbands, as our newspapers sometimes reveal. A well-known, wealthy Long Island woman shot her husband dead some years ago, claiming she thought he was a burglar stealing into their home early in the morning. She was not given a prison sentence, although later it was revealed that her husband was leaving her for another woman and had been having affairs for years.

George Bernard Shaw, in his 1911 play *Getting Married,* wrote: "When two people are under the influence of the most violent, most insane, most delusive, and most transient of passions, they are required to swear that they will retain that excited, abnormal, and exhausting condition continuously until death do them part."

Such imagined bliss at the start of a love affair or marriage has, in our country, ended in divorce for more than half the marriages. In addition, hundreds of thousands of couples live separately, not divorced. Many take on other partners. As one husband told his therapist, "Why should I marry again and risk the same unhappy ending? I might as well live with someone and hope we'll get along without the fights that seem to be part of marriage."

Does marriage, in so many instances, *have* to lead to hatred and murder? Is wishing to live "happily ever after" pure fantasy? Should we give up the idea that a marriage can exist without hatred, without the strong wish to kill the partner at times? Without, in many instances, actual murder?

Since the start of recorded history, marriage has been an essential institution in virtually every society known to humankind. Yet despite the ubiquity of marriage since the beginning of civilization, there has never been what we might call a Golden Age of marriage. When Adam and

Eve brought sex into their marriage, they were banished from the Garden of Eden and their fighting probably started. Their hostility may have been so intense that their inability to provide a loving climate in their home resulted in one son murdering the other. The deeds of children reflect the violence they witness their parents acting out.

Abraham was so smitten by the idea of God that he seriously neglected his wife, Sarah. It is also clear that hatred was pervasive between kings and the queens they selected to marry; in addition, many a king had a harem, which meant his women would be very jealous of one another. Because a king possessed so many women, his sexual demands on any one would doubtless be minimal, so women turned to each other to relieve their sexual desire.

The history of marriage thus shows a sorrowful picture as "love at first sight" often swiftly turns into "hatred at second sight." While statistics may reveal that wife-beating by husbands appears rampant, they also show that 20 percent of American wives beat their husbands. In his recent book *The Meaning of Love in Human Experience*, Reuben Fine points out that in his extensive examination of many cultures, past and present, "marriage is war" in most.

To fuse tender and erotic feelings in a marriage seems for many men and women to be close to a gigantic and impossible task—one that many couples conclude lies beyond their powers. The hate that soon develops for the partner appears to throttle all feelings of passion, love, devotion, and friendship.

Though many societies over the ages have idealized marriage, few societies can point to a successful marital structure. From the Bible we know Paul advocated celibacy and deprecated marriage. St. Jerome averred that the man who ardently loves his wife should be viewed as an adulterer. When the ancient Greeks tried open marriage, the result was an increase in homosexuality and a decrease in heterosexual alliances. Palladas, a poet of ancient Greece, expressed an opinion about marriage that many men had at the time and still do: "Marriage brings a man only two happy days: the day he takes his bride to bed and the day he lays her in her grave."

Socially it is more acceptable for a man to be unfaithful than a woman. Many believe men are more inclined to be unfaithful because women are dependent economically on a man and don't want to jeopardize their monetary security. Society has viewed the straying wife more punitively than the straying husband. He has gone unpunished over the years by the law.

Dr. Ernest Jones, one of the world's foremost psychoanalysts, said in the late 1950s, "Every form of marriage so far attempted has been accompanied by serious disadvantages. Polygamy, monogamy, easy divorce: none provides a satisfactory solution." Like many writers, Jones was making an autobiographical statement. He personally found marriage very difficult—he married three times.

Dr. Karen Horney, a creative psychoanalyst, wrote a paper in the 1920s called "The Problems of the Monogamous Ideal." She expressed the belief that man's state of mind does not allow the possibility of a warm, loving monogamous relationship. But she may have been slightly influenced by growing up in a household where her father was almost never present. He was captain of a ship that was usually at sea, on the way to some far port.

In her paper Horney concluded: "It never has been and never will be possible to find any principle that will solve the conflicts of married life." Like Jones, Horney suffered during two marriages.

Incidentally, there is no reason why some psychologists and psychiatrists such as Ernest Jones and Karen Horney should not have troubled marriages, for they are human too. Even though many have faced themselves in their own personal psychotherapy—required for legitimate clinicians—they, too, find it difficult to fuse tender and erotic wishes.

Most men and women feel that it is better to marry and fail—even several times—than never to marry at all. The spinster is looked upon as a freak and the bachelor as an asexual celibate. While neither of these stereotypes is ac- curate, our society still champions marriage and tends to look askance at those who remain unmarried.

As a rule, the unmarried not only fear their own sexual feelings but wish to avoid the quarreling and the disap- pointment they are aware occurs in most marriages. Any serious look at marriage as a way of life shows that most men and women who do marry wind up hating each other much of the time.

Since the beginning of recorded time, starting with Adam and Eve and persisting into the 1990s, marriage has al- ways been idealized. Regardless of the particular society and of the period of history, we consider a man without a woman like a door without a key. Songs proliferate on this theme, including "For Every Man There's a Woman." The lyrics in another song tell us, "Love and marriage, love and marriage, go together like a horse and carriage."

No society idealizes loneliness. In this country only one bachelor, James Buchanan, has ever been elected Presi- dent, and probably no other will be for the next one hun- dred years. Marriage is a powerful social, religious, and psychological phenomenon that has remained constant since the first man and woman on earth.

In spite of our disillusionment with marriage, we still extol the fantasy of "love and marriage" and link them to- gether. At the onset of a relationship, most of us fall under the spell of the idea of romantic love that originated in the twelfth century in France. We still esteem and fantasize about the great lovers—Romeo and Juliet, Tristan and Is- olde, Antony and Cleopatra. We ardently hope we may find a romance similar to the ones they were alleged to have enjoyed.

But there is one fact we do not take into account. Every one of these historic loving couples lived apart. They ide- alized each other in their fantasies without the curse of reality setting in. Romeo never saw Juliet in curlers. Juliet never heard Romeo snore next to her in bed.

Like all men and women who fall "desperately" in love, the great lovers of history could extravagantly praise the objects of their passion from a distance. Because, as far as we know, they never actually lived with each other, they avoided the inevitable trials and tribulations that lead to hatred and the wish to murder in marriage.

From the time of ancient romantics, in which the loved one was believed to be an asexual person, to the start of the twentieth century, almost every statement about marriage suggests rather strongly that it is not "womanly" for the wife to display her sexual feelings. It has been only within the last few decades that society has permitted women to think of themselves as the sexual equals of men.

If we examine the history of Babylon and Egypt, we find a consistent subjugation of women. They were originally treated as third-class citizens, particularly in marital relationships. If a husband died, the woman was killed and buried with him. Even today in Brazil, for instance, as our newspapers and television tell us, husbands receive no jail sentence for murdering an unfaithful wife.

Although the women's movement, psychoanalysis, education, and the current sexual revolution have tended to encourage the notion that those who marry are entitled to equal rights, marriage still remains a power struggle and a murderous state of mind for many. The desire to be the most powerful one in the marriage is a strong wish from childhood, when the child felt powerless and often the sufferer. Furthermore, the child also is apt to witness over the years many struggles between his mother and father to be the powerful one of the family.

"This marriage thing is a breeze," announced a young policeman, returning from his honeymoon. He was speaking to his colleagues at the police station during an episode of "Cagney and Lacey" on television. Whereupon a veteran woman police officer said sarcastically, "Just give it time, sugar."

"Time" appears to erode love in marriage as fantasy expectations turn to dust. Slowly, in many cases not so slowly, the expectations of a heavenly relationship are shattered as the relationship becomes a living hell. Neither partner can understand why this has happened.

When the fantasies of both the man and the woman repeatedly get punctured, they become increasingly alienated. The major factor in the deterioration of a marriage is that neither partner can possibly be perfect. No one can fulfill his own wish to be perfect or expect perfection from anyone else. Marriage also tends to induce regression. All husbands and wives carry with them the buried wish to be little children. This means they feel insatiable and will never be satisfied—by anyone.

Men are abused more subtly than women. Many times a woman will make a derogatory remark about a man's loss of sexual competence or call him a poor breadwinner or a bad sport. Women also express their contempt and rage by being cold and withholding sex or never showing appreciation, also a form of abuse.

Couples have tried many arrangements without success. Compromise marriage. Open marriage. Conventional marriage. Living together without marrying to find out if they are compatible. Bisexual marriage. Homosexual marriage. Celibate marriage.

Perhaps unfortunately the reality of marriage was best stated by the eloquent spokesman Groucho Marx, who once said, "Marriage is a wonderful institution—provided you like to live in an institution."

Despite the fact that our divorce rate is higher than ever, men and women still idealize marriage. They race into it, ignore its known limitations. The pressure of parents and society is placed on young people to marry as early as they can, but actually the age of marriage keeps getting higher. This is prolongation of adolescence. Very few seem to want to ask themselves why so many marriages end in hate and the wish to kill the partner, if not in actual violence and murder.

Some are able to be honest about their feelings. One husband at his wife's funeral (she died of cancer, not from his murderous attack) saw a man he did not know, standing by the casket, tears running down his face. The husband realized the stranger must be his wife's lover, about whom she had talked. He walked over to the man, put his arm around him and said with compassion, "Don't worry. I'll get married again."

The novelist John O'Hara wrote, "A married couple always present an absurd and untruthful picture to the world but it is a picture the world finds convenient and a comfort."

Such falsity becomes apparent in those men and women who seek a therapist after marriage to relieve their raging, murderous feelings. It comes as no surprise to the therapist how very unhappy most married couples are. He is aware that studies of marriage overlook the disillusioning fact that every normal person is stirred by deep conflicts that become even more unbearable in marriage. The act of two people intimately living together sets fire to the fantasies that for years have remained hidden and supposedly "safe" from explosion.

One woman of thirty-five, an advertising executive, sought a psychotherapist after a marriage of five years to a Wall Street broker. The first words out of her mouth in the therapist's office were, "I knew I shouldn't have married the son of a bitch. It hit me the moment we marched down the aisle as I fully realized his overbearing manner."

She was silent a few moments, then went on. "I admit I married him because I didn't want to be the only unmarried child in the family. My three sisters all married years ago. I thought my husband might change some of his stubborn ways." She sighed. "I stood it five years. But when our sex life became for the birds, I gave up. I'm here for help. Sometimes I feel so desperate I am afraid I will kill him or myself if I stay with him."

Sociological studies of any community—past or present—show that more than 80 percent of men and women battle deep emotional conflicts. When two individuals with serious personal problems marry, it is inevitable that this will be a very disturbed and hateful marriage.

It has become a psychological axiom that if you are unhappy when you marry, believing the marriage will solve all problems, you are doomed to hate your spouse sooner or later. Mostly sooner. All of us are unhappy to some degree, some of us more than others. Life cannot possibly fulfill the fantasies that whirl around the act of marriage.

A moderately happy person will choose another moderately happy person and have a moderately happy marriage. An unhappy person will choose an unhappy partner and face an unhappy marriage. But most unhappy men and women do not realize the depth of the hatred that has existed in their hearts from childhood on. They ascribe their hatred to others, feel they are the victims of other people's rage. In marriage they do the same—their partners are vilified and condemned, told repeatedly how sadistic they are.

This is shown in a humorous but deadly way by mystery writer Mary Higgins Clark, who says that when an Irishman proposes, he asks his beloved sweetheart not "Will you marry me, luv?" but "Do you want to be buried next to my mother?"

Perhaps our blindness to the anger we carry with us from childhood into marriage is part of nature's way of insuring that the human race will continue. If we all knew in advance that our murderous wishes would emerge after marrying, probably we would never marry and bear children and this would end the human race.

We know, from countless psychological studies, that the deeper the anger we felt at our parents as we grew up, the deeper the anger we inflict on a spouse. Children brought up by thoughtful and loving mothers and fathers will, as adults, accept the limitations of being human. If they do not strive to be gods or expect their partners to be perfect, they will not feel murderous fury in marriage. Unfortunately, we venture the guess that only about 5 percent of the population meets these criteria.

The hatred that can exist in marriage was described by a twenty-nine-year-old woman who consulted a therapist. She told him that she absolutely "loathed" her husband, the owner of a large advertising agency, though she never told him this. Instead she suffered, explaining, "He watches wrestling on television almost every night. He's a vicious man, as vicious as a hungry tiger. He cheers for one wrestler to kill the other."

One day as she started to repeat these charges, she said in a voice filled with hate, "Anybody who watches wrestling ought to be shot!" Thus she revealed that she wished her husband dead. She showed that underneath her criticism lay a sadism as strong as her husband's. As inevitably as the sun rises each day, every sadistic man finds an outwardly masochistic woman to marry and vice versa. Sometimes the couple's similarities are obscured but every marriage without exception consists of two individuals at about the same level of emotional maturity.

One woman, outwardly quiet and placid, married a man who within weeks started to drink heavily. Within months he lost control and beat her so cruelly there were nights she fled to a hotel, her eyes blackened, her face bruised. She sought a woman therapist who eventually could tell her, after hearing more of her life, "You unconsciously chose someone who would act out your rage for you." As a child, both of her parents would fight continually, sometimes turning their wrath on her.

"Why, I'm not an angry person!" the woman said, surprised. "Everyone praises me for my peaceful manner."

"You have hidden your anger successfully," the therapist said. "Both from others and yourself."

As the therapy progressed, this woman, an executive in a large department store, realized that over the years she had denied an intense fury toward her mother, an overpossessive, dominating woman, and her father, who showed the same need to control everyone else. As a child she had learned to hold back all anger, never defying her parents' wishes. The man she chose to marry displayed the rage she wished she could have shown earlier in life but had been too afraid to admit consciously. Instead, she married a cruel man who would express anger for her—a very frequent, perhaps to some degree a universal phenomenon in marriage.

The reverse is also true. One husband constantly complained how embarrassed he felt when his wife told off-color jokes. Later he discovered one of the reasons he married her was that he secretly admired what she could courageously express but which appeared forbidden to him. A wife who constantly complained that her husband was always dirty, showered infrequently, and "smelled like a pig pen," eventually discovered how much she resented her mother for always reminding her as a young girl that "cleanliness is next to godliness."

A married couple who hate each other need to realize they write their own emotional scripts. Most angry spouses cling to the belief they are the victim of a hateful partner and if they only were married to someone else, miraculously they would live in happiness.

But there are no miracles in marriage. Marriage requires much wisdom, much maturity, much tolerance, much empathy, much forgiveness, and much acceptance of frustration. For a marriage to endure happily both partners must monitor their mutual hatreds and master their unrealistic childish wishes for perfection, for bliss, for a paradise that does not exist.

When marriages are full of strife, each partner has to understand that he is in large part still an angry child demanding more than is humanly possible for a mate to deliver. And that the same hatred will probably emerge if he makes a second, third, or fourth marriage. There are no innocent victims or guilty abusers when violence appears in marriage. Each partner must be aware of the fury within himself and control the universal tendency to ascribe unhappiness to the spouse.

A man of forty-two, a wealthy real-estate broker, told his therapist after several months, "I never realized my murderous feelings toward my wife were originally directed at my strict, harsh mother of childhood. Now I look at my wife, whose mother is also an impossible person, with more understanding and love. Maybe we'll eventually make it together." The wife was also seeing a counselor in an attempt to save the marriage.

We cannot expect our mates to be the perfect parents we never had. We should understand there is no reason for anger when they are unable to assume this unrealistic role. Each partner has to accept the thought that when he feels murderous, in essence he has become the infant who cannot get what he wants the minute he wants it.

A male patient, a writer of mystery stories, thirty-eight years old, said of his wife, a fashion designer, "She's the most controlling bitch I've ever seen. Why didn't I recognize this *before* I married her?" In anger, he continued, "She's just like my mother. In everything she does. Even says."

At this point he laughed. Then he explained, "I know by now, I was destined to pick a gal just like my mom."

Each marital partner, when unhappy and angry, would do well to ask, "How does venting my anger help the relationship?" And should realize in most cases it will not, though sometimes helpful dialogues conducted in a sympathetic tone may ease the hatred and add to the understanding of each other's conflicts.

A woman of twenty-nine, a lawyer, told her marriage counselor, "I have convinced my husband, when he gets angry, that instead of drinking vodka by the pint and then hitting me, it is a good idea to sit down and tell me what bothers him. He is just beginning to understand that his anger is not at me but, as he says, his 'crazy mother.' "

She confessed, a few months later, "I couldn't really understand my husband until I understood my own childhood hatred. Then I could sympathize with what he had gone through. His mother really was crazy. She had been in a mental institution at one time for over a year."

Marriages choked by hatred may change to understanding, then caring about the partner, if the incessant "unreal" demands on each other become diminished. Each must face the threats from the other that spark rage, rather than react to them. Then they must understand why they want to react so strongly to the threats. We do not feel murderous toward a partner unless he touches off a buried anger in our lives that originated between us and our mother and/or father and/or siblings.

All the anxiety and all the resentments toward our parents we have buried over the years are often shot out verbally at the marital partner. We feel like murdering our "parent-spouse" for our own childhood hurts and indignities. In extramarital affairs defiance of the spouse is always present. Rebellion against rules and regulations is always present. Shame and embarrassment because of sexual fantasies toward parental figures are always present.

The adulterer is an angry child who can only feel sexually secure away from "home and mother" or father. Rarely does the participant in an extramarital affair realize how much of an unhappy, angry child he still is. Like an irresponsible child he projects the marital difficulties onto the partner and feels self-righteous about his neurotic behavior.

A phenomenon that has become quite popular during the last two or three decades is that of a couple living together unmarried. Fearing the commitment of marriage, many believe they can get along reasonably well providing they do not feel bound by the controls marriage imposes. But many of those who enjoy each other while living together seem to become hateful, even murderous, after marrying.

As long as they are not married, they do not feel as if they are confined children. But when they marry, like most married persons they turn their partners into parental figures, seeing them as domineering and controlling. They feel pressured and oppressed. A hatred for their partner thus develops. Sex becomes far less a pleasure for the man who is now a husband but feels he is in bed with his mother. The wife feels she is sleeping with her father.

Happy men and women accept reality and are not burdened by unrealistic demands on themselves or their spouse. Happy people accept the fact that life, the spouse, and they themselves are all imperfect. Most unhappy people chase rainbows and cannot accept life's limitations.

PART 4

The Most Desperate Murders

8

Murder in the Heart of the Serial Killer

"As Konrad Lorenz has shown, of all the carnivores, only two lack built-in inhibitions against killing members of their own species—rats and man."

—*John Bartlow Martin*

A young man named Jürgen Bartsch spent his twenty-second birthday in November 1969 in a prison cell in Duisberg, Germany. A year before, the German magazine *Der Stern* had published the results of a poll conducted by the organization Infratest to determine not only the "darlings of the nation" but "this century's greatest criminal."

In the latter category, not surprisingly, Hitler took first place. Second place went to young Bartsch. Paul Moor, American author and journalist, attended Bartsch's trial in Wuppertal. After it ended he wrote *The Self-Portrait of Jürgen Bartsch*, published by Rowohlt in Germany in 1972. He has just finished a completely new full-length account of the murders, also to be published in Germany by Rowohlt in 1991. It is one of the most revealing books on why a murderer is driven to kill.

Bartsch is probably the youngest serial killer, at least the youngest ever caught. At fifteen he committed his first murder of a youth. By the time he was arrested at eighteen, he had killed four more boys, burying them in a cave near his home, after cutting them to bits. His sixth attempt went awry. This time the victim managed to escape from the cave after Bartsch tied him up, planning to return later for the kill. The details the victim gave police led to Bartsch's arrest the following day.

Interviewed by Lucy Freeman for this book, Moor described a paper he wrote at the time of the first trial, "Jürgen Bartsch: Human, All Too Human." Moor told how he set about finding out as much as he could of Bartsch's childhood, later revealed in his book. Moor had been psychoanalyzed in Berlin and knew that if we are treated in childhood with hatred and violence, such treatment sets the stage for our later emotional behavior. He wanted to find out what violent cruelties existed in Bartsch's childhood that drove him at such an early age to become a serial killer of young boys.

Moor quoted from an essay on the criminal mentality by John Bartlow Martin: "As Konrad Lorenz has shown, of all the carnivores, only two lack built-in inhibitions against killing members of their own species—rats and man. All human societies distinguish between killing members of one's own group and killing outsiders. The latter is called 'warfare'; the former, 'murder.'"

Moor told Freeman, "Since man does not feel inhibited against killing his own kind, he has enacted laws against it. We punish murder. Nevertheless, we feel fairly comfortable with murder for profit, or revenge, or jealousy. What shocks us is a murder 'without reason.'"

He set out to find the "reason" why young Bartsch became a serial killer, interviewing him in prison. The book is researched in psychological depth and shows without a doubt that young Bartsch never had a chance to become normal. As Moor said,

> To derive any real insight into the probably unique personality of Jürgen Bartsch, in which an extraordinarily violent species of sadism, stopping just short of cannibalism, combined with such further disorders

as paedophilia and necrophilia, to contort an intelligent, polite, well-spoken, likeable but indescribably lonely and unhappy fifteen-year-old into a murderer of almost incredible violence and cruelty, one had to listen with the most intense concentration not only to every word but to every syllable, and one often had to pay even closer attention to things that did not get said.

Jürgen Bartsch never knew his parents. He was born on November 6, 1946, the illegitimate son of a tubercular war widow and an itinerant Dutch worker. His mother abandoned him after birth in the hospital as she secretly left, prior to being discharged. He spent the first months of his life in the hospital, cared for by nurses, like Joseph Kallinger, Son of Sam, and Theodore Bundy. For Bartsch it was six months.

At this time, Gertrud Bartsch, wife of a prosperous butcher in Essen, entered the same hospital to undergo an operation that left her unable to have a child. She and her husband decided to take the infant Bartsch into their home, adopted him legally seven years later.

According to Moor, "His new parents, throughout his formative years, kept him strictly and completely isolated, at all times and without exception, from all other children to prevent his learning they had adopted him." His father opened a second butcher shop so his son would have his own shop as early as possible. Gertrud went to work there, leaving first her mother, then a succession of hired girls to look after the boy.

When he was ten, his Catholic parents sent him to a small school where he had a reasonably pleasant environment, but then, at twelve, they took him to a Catholic school where three hundred boys, many of them serious problems to their parents, lived together under strict, even harsh military discipline. He told Moor one of the priests seduced him.

Between 1962, when he was fifteen, and 1966, Bartsch

killed five boys and estimated he made perhaps one hundred further attempts at a homicidally intended pickup, which went awry. He tried to persuade his victims, usually on the pretext of buried treasure and weapons, to accompany him into his cave—a long, dark shaft drilled horizontally into a hillside that had been used as a bomb shelter during World War II but abandoned long since. The bunker lay at the foot of the high hill atop which his parents had their home.

According to Moor, after overpowering and beating his victim into submission, too far inside the cave for any passersby to hear the screams, Bartsch would tie him tightly with fine, strong cord, manipulate the boy's genitals while he masturbated, then kill the boy by strangulation or bludgeoning. After this, he would open the body, empty the abdominal and breast cavities, and bury the remains.

During his testimony he repeatedly stressed that he had derived his most profound sexual pleasure and gratification not from the masturbation but from the cutting, which brought him to spontaneous orgasms. (It is possible he had seen the cutting of animal flesh ever since he was a small child in the two butcher shops run by his parents, one by his father, the other by his mother. The wielding of the butcher's knife and the bloody flesh of animals somehow become entwined in his distorted mind with the sexual impulse.)

In his interview for this book Moor said, "Jürgen Bartsch did not enter this vale of tears as the psychopathic murderer he became. . . . One must begin by looking inside the home of the Bartsches in Langenfeld as experienced by the three human beings who lived there in such a bewildering mixture of intimacy and self-concealment."

His adoptive mother, as he grew up, vacillated between being seductive and violent. She bathed him until he was eighteen, touching his body all over with her soapy hands, no doubt stimulating him sexually. But she also threw knives at him when he disobeyed, knives he learned to duck (the knife used as a weapon to slaughter a little boy).

He said at the trial he never "got love" from his mother or father, that "my parents always had a little bit less than too little time for me."

Bartsch told Moor that shortly after his eighth birthday he had his first homosexual experience when a relative twice his age commanded him to lie down on the couch and open his trousers, in exchange for allowing him to listen to the radio through the older boy's earphones. Of this overpowering seduction, Bartsch said only, "I just thought he wasn't quite all there."

He ran away twice from the cruel Catholic school for boys, the second time with his only friend, Detlev, whom he tried, for his first murder, to seduce and kill. He thought that if he killed Detlev he would no longer reject his sexual advances. Bartsch never went beyond this statement, which shows how emotionally ill he was.

Moor points out that during the trial Bartsch made an intricate and interesting slip of the tongue, mixing two German expressions, one meaning to hang on to the tassels of a mother's apron string, the other referring to a mama's boy. Many Germans used the word for tassel, *Zipfel,* as a euphemism for a child's penis. Moor says, "As Bartsch stammered out his inadvertent mixture of the two phrases, he revealed himself simultaneously not only as a mama's boy, hanging on to her apron strings, but also hanging on to a child's penis."

Undoubtedly, many times in his early life, as his mother threatened to punish him, he feared she would cut off his penis when she threw a knife at him. As he later cut up the boys he attacked, he was telling the world of his acute fear for his own life at the hands of a violent parent. Many a little boy whose mother screams at him may be seen clutching his penis as though to protect it.

Bartsch saw no love in his parents, either for himself or for each other. "Hardly a day passed without their yelling at each other," he told Moor. "It was usually about money. My mother at one period wanted to run away. She once thought seriously of getting a divorce and even went to consult a lawyer."

When the judge asked which parent played the dominant role, Bartsch replied, "My mother carries the greater weight. I've often seen my father sit on the bed and weep." He said his mother always chose his clothes as his father would say scornfully, "You can't even dress yourself alone."

Bartsch told Moor his mother bathed him "all over—right up to the day the police came," when he was eighteen. Moor comments, "The phrase 'all over,' from which he refused to budge during the trial, became particularly important in later testimony."

Day in, day out, Bartsch said, his evenings consisted of his mother's bathing him, after which he would put on his pajamas in his parents' bedroom (his own room, directly overhead, had neither closet nor washbasin). He would watch television as he lay between them in their bed, which stimulated him sexually. He managed nocturnal excursions by slipping out a cellar window in his pajamas, changing into clothes he had cached in a nearby culvert.

He described his father alternately as a "work-horse" and a "top-sergeant type," calling him "very loud." He added, "Whenever we visited relatives, he always ran me down in front of them. I never had any trust in either one of my parents."

If a child grows up with a parent who runs him down and whom he does not trust, Moor noted, he is apt to become a very hostile child—one who hates the parent, hates himself, is unable to show tenderness to anyone. His sexual development is apt to be warped; his normal sexual desire remains that of a primitive, furious, emotionally deprived small child who wants only to scream, lash out and kill.

According to Bartsch, only once did he ever have a conversation with his father about sexual matters, and by that time the boy's psychic life "had become far sicker than his father or almost anyone else would have believed," Moor said.

Bartsch told the court, "My father and I just didn't fit together. Anyway, I never amounted to anything special as an apprentice butcher." Except perhaps to use a knife to cut both animal and human flesh apart.

He learned only at the age of thirteen that he was adopted. He began smoking at fifteen, drinking at seventeen. Not infrequently he drank up to twenty cognacs during the course of his secret evenings away from home. At eighteen he was picked up by police for drunken driving, lost his driver's license for four months, and spent three weeks in jail.

A very important point was made when his parents admitted that he had slept in their room until he was five or six. Being constantly present all night in the room of parents is very anxiety-provoking to a child. Son of Sam, the New York killer of couples parked in cars, also went through this emotional torture (the young men and women making love obviously represented his parents of the earlier days). Bartsch had no conscious recollection of the primal scene, having repressed all his terrifying memories, as children do.

In his teens he tried to have sex with girls "but his inexorable timidity prevented any progress in the relationship," Moor said. "During all these almost frenzied undertakings, just as earlier, he had no one to whom he could turn for sensible help or even for compassionate understanding."

Moor also pointed out that when we look at the details of the five murders and the sixth attempted one, which led to Bartsch's apprehension, we notice "not only a diminution of his inhibitions but also an increase in his carelessness and even foolhardiness, which from the psychopathological standpoint one must regard as a desperate inner wish for someone to catch him and put an end to his killing."

Bartsch's downfall came on June 18, 1966, when he enticed fourteen-year-old Peter Frese into the cave, beat and bound him, and left him there in order to appear punctually at home "for this stupid, heavy soup I always had to eat," so his mother would not scold him for being late or absent. He had left Peter one burning candle for warmth.

Although somewhat mentally retarded, Peter had seen enough movies and television programs to know what to do. He burned the bonds off his ankles, managed to clothe himself at least partially and escape. When Bartsch returned after supper to complete his interrupted sadism and found Peter gone, he first reacted, as he described it during the trial, with the disappointment of someone who has started something pleasurable and then been unable to finish it.

Though Bartsch must have known Peter's escape would inevitably lead to his arrest, he set out three days later to look for another boy. When the judge exclaimed over this cold-blooded act, Bartsch replied, according to Moor, "in a tone that made it clear he hardly could have acted differently and that anyone ought to comprehend so irresistible a drive, 'I was still completely unsatisfied.' "

When the judge at another point asked whether Bartsch's acts had ever horrified him, he heaved a long sigh. Finally he said in a tone of sheer desperation, "Your Honor, that would presuppose that I could regulate things—now you can, now you can't. But I couldn't regulate them." Meaning he had no control over his violent or sexual feelings—they controlled him.

When Gerhard Bartsch, the adoptive father, took the stand, he admitted that he and his wife had made a mistake in never allowing their son to play with other children and keeping the fact of his adoption from him until he was thirteen—the time he committed his first murder, as though telling the world he did not care from now on what happened to him, he had endured enough suffering.

Gerhard Bartsch also described his years as a sergeant during World War II as "the happiest years of my life," showing the large part sadism and violence played in the father's mind. We know young Bartsch had a violent mother and we may assume his father, although he did not display outright violence, kept it tightly guarded near the surface of his mind.

The father described on the stand how his son worked first for a friend's butcher shop, then for his shop, where he kept the boy busy. He said, "Sixty hours a week isn't too much for a sixteen-year-old. He wasn't just some apprentice from the outside, he was my son." Meaning he could work the boy as hard as he wished. Bartsch commented, "In my father's shop I had things worse in every way. I had no free time at all anymore."

The reports of three neurologists called by the court as "expert witnesses" received much attention during the trial. They were almost totally unfavorable to the youth, Moor told Freeman, "almost as if the neurologists had taken the duties of the prosecution upon themselves." They emphasized that any prognosis for surgical or hormonal castration must remain speculative because cases of relapse had occurred.

When asked after his arrest if he could commit such murders again, Bartsch answered in "breathtaking honesty" with the word "yes," Moor revealed.

One expert mentioned that Bartsch had become toilet-trained at fifteen months. When the judge questioned this early an age, Bartsch replied, "My mother will have beaten that into me. She's broken more than one wooden clothes hanger across my back."

Such early violence by a mother, as we know now, almost ensures that a child will copy her and become a violent adolescent, then adult. Children use their parents as models—both the evil in them and the good.

Moor said he had found out that until Bartsch grew big enough to offer formidable resistance, he had received frequent corporal punishment, almost always from his mother, who usually favored wooden coat hangers as her weapon. He was often punished for inconsequential offenses, such as coming into the house with unclean shoes (many Germans are noted for their emphasis on "cleanliness," as though outer cleanliness directs attention away from "inner" dirty thoughts and wishes).

Moor pointed out, "punishment often had its origin in Frau Bartsch's momentary mood, which could do a complete about-face in a split second. The expressions she employed in speaking of Jürgen—most of them had to do with the golden hair he had as an infant—indicated that she had found him a comely object but revealed little inner feeling toward the child as a person."

He noted that "one glimpse of Frau Bartsch's personality emerged when it transpired during testimony that after Jürgen's arrest a number of former customers stopped buying meat from the Bartsches. When the daughter of one such customer died and the daughter of another turned to prostitution, Frau Bartsch remarked with satisfaction that the mothers had received their 'just deserts.' A glimpse into Jürgen Bartsch came with his reaction to his mother's vicious statement: he found her completely illogical."

The illogical way she had acted toward him all his life, particularly when he was a small child, distorted his entire perspective of reality. It was as though he had been brought up by inmates of an insane asylum, both his aggressive and sexual drives warped beyond all control.

Dr. Benjamin Karpman, a psychiatrist, writes in *The Sexual Offender and His Offenses* that the perpetrators of purely sadistic homicides or "lust murders" are "nearly always psychotic and many of them are sexually impotent." Dr. Otto Fenichel in *The Psychoanalytic Theory of Neurosis* says, "If sexual pleasure is disturbed by anxiety it is comprehensible that an identification with the aggressor can be a relief. If a person is able to do to others what he fears may be done to him, he no longer has to be afraid. Anything that tends to increase his power or prestige can be used as a reassurance against anxieties. What might happen to him passively is done actively by him, in anticipation of attack by others."

Moor described Frau Bartsch as a short, stout woman,

who appeared in court wearing galoshes, a black fur coat, and a serviceable hat pulled down over her white hair. She seemed on the verge of tears most of the time. The judge asked whether she reproached herself for having devoted more time and attention to the butcher shop than to the rearing of her son. She cried out, "No! Not at all! The shop was my very existence! Thousands of families have it just the same way!"

She said she insisted on an early curfew for her son even when he reached his teens "because in my eyes he wasn't grown up at all. When he came from work, he had to check in with me so I'd know nothing had happened." She described what was now her twenty-one-year-old son as "still just a big kid." She had infantilized him to a severe degree, which meant his sexual and violent feelings were still intertwined as they are naturally in small children.

Moor recalled that the judge asked with a deprecating smile and jocular tone about the stories of her bathing her son right up to the day of the arrest. She sniffed at such reports as "ridiculous." She added, "I never felt anything at all when I bathed him," replying to a question the judge probably would not have dared ask. She went on, "I've never noticed that a boy his age"—he was eighteen when arrested—"really gets himself clean. I washed his head and back, but not his private parts." Even if she did not touch the latter, both son and mother would be well aware they were visible and arousing forbidden feelings within both.

It is significant that Bartsch murdered his fifth and last victim on Mother's Day in 1966, returning home at nine P.M. When the judge asked if she was annoyed at his lateness Frau Bartsch replied, "Yes, extremely." The judge then wanted to know if she had seen any blood spots on the cuff of his shirt, which he had reported were there. She responded with what Moor called a "fascinating switch of verbs" in the words, "No, I didn't hear anything of that," transposing "seen" into "hear"—one cannot "hear" blood spots.

At the press table in front of where Moor sat during the trial, he recalled hearing an older, seasoned reporter ask a younger, studious-looking colleague, "What do you think of the mother?"

The younger man, gathering together his papers, thought a moment, then replied, "The female who eats her young."

This seemed an apt description of the emotional way Frau Bartsch had destroyed an important part of the child she brought up, through her violence and lack of awareness of what he needed to be nurtured properly. Her clinging to him physically and psychologically, then threatening at times to kill him, sounded his death knell. She in turn must have had a similarly traumatic childhood.

The court tried Bartsch as an adult and sentenced him to life imprisonment. At one point he wrote a letter to the parents of a boy he had murdered, saying, "I have taken from you what was dearest on earth to you." Moor raised the point that just as every suicide substitutes in reality for a murder of one or more persons against whom the suicide directs his repressed rage, to some extent Bartsch's five murders represented the disguised killings of the two parents who had "brought him up with love and goodness," as they said.

Moor showed Freeman copies of Bartsch's suicide letters, which Moor had sent to Professor Tobias Brocher of the Frankfurt Sigmund Freud Institute after Brocher had written in the *Frankfurter Rundschau:* "What the assailant actually seeks in his victim is an image of himself as a child, which he can then ruin and destroy just as he himself as a child was destroyed. This is the unconscious content of Bartsch's revenge, which he today terms his 'uncanny, sinister drive' without actually knowing what it is."

Moor noted that his experiences in Wuppertal impelled him to reread the book *Father Land* by Dr. Bertram Schaffner, a New York psychoanalyst who in 1946 conducted an extensive study of the authoritarian pattern in the German family structure with particular emphasis on child-rearing. Moor believed many passages aptly apply to the Bartsch case.

Schaffner almost draws a portrait from life of the Bartsch family, Moor pointed out, when he writes:

> At few points, if any, does the typical German child come to know the meaning of freedom. His own free fantasy is discouraged by the system of training and eduction. . . . The child is not taught to express himself as an individual but to make himself like the German ideal. . . . He is thereby deprived of much of his own initiative. . . . The children are not only denied freedom but induced not to want it.

Moor concluded that Bartsch emerged from a German environment that seems almost a caricature of "good" and "typical," that "the savagery of the psychological wounds it dealt him during his formative years, for which no one can hold the child responsible, shows its measure in the savagery which he in turn vented upon his own victims."

He continued:

> The traditional, unchanged German family pattern of authoritarianism which produced the sadistic murderers of the Bialystok Jews also produced, in our own day, Jürgen Bartsch, and this traditional progression, largely unaltered, perpetuates itself still in many less enlightened German families today. As George Santayana once observed, "He who refuses to learn from history is condemned to repeat it."

The Bartsch case in Germany and the serial murders that have occurred in other countries, including our own, show that as long as we continue to ignore the cruel and sadistic sexual and aggressive treatment of children, we will continue to produce serial murderers—as well as murderers of all kinds, who take revenge on the innocent for the severe punishment the killers suffered in childhood.

This is their way of trying to show the world what was "done unto them." They fight against their strong unconscious feelings of infantile anxiety, hate and wish for revenge by threatening or murdering others who cannot fight back, as they could not fight their giant parents.

Moor was impressed by the fact that Bartsch "did not try to hide anything. Once the damn broke he was just as eager to find out what had caused him to become a serial killer as the court was. He became desperately eager to tell absolutely everything in his writings. He showed a gift in writing."

The young Bartsch's "normal feelings" had been destroyed by his cruel foster parents. They stirred within him an anger so intense he literally ripped apart young boys as he himself felt ripped apart by the two strangers, who called themselves his mother and his father, as he grew up in a house of violence and hatred.

In America, Theodore Bundy recently became famous as a serial killer. He was held in prison ten years before being electrocuted in Starke, Florida, on January 24, 1989. He was convicted of three murders, the last a twelve-year-old girl in Florida. He died at forty-two, nearly fifteen years after he embarked on a trail of murders throughout the Northwest, California, and Florida, the state to which he fled after breaking out of jail.

He made a plea for his life when interviewed on September 24, 1989, by Maury Povich for "A Current Affair." He said the nation might profit if he was allowed to live and tell a psychoanalyst what he thought had driven him to serial murders so they might be prevented.

An illuminating article by Myra MacPherson, "The Roots of Evil," appeared in the May 1989 *Vanity Fair.* MacPherson interviewed Dr. Dorothy Lewis, a New York psychiatrist, who had seen Bundy during his last hours. What she discovered was quite different from his mother's story of a normal childhood and adolescence and Bundy's claim that "pornography" in the home as he grew up was to blame for his lust and murderous feelings.

His mother, Louise, the oldest of three sisters, had "an explosive temper," just like her father, according to MacPherson. The father, a man who allowed no one to disagree with him, struck his wife at times. Bundy's grandmother lived with the family and was repeatedly taken to the hospital for shock treatments because of depression.

Bundy's great-aunt, Virginia Bristol, told Dr. Lewis that Louise's father, Sam Cowell, was feared by his own brothers, one of whom stated, "I always thought he was crazy." According to one of Bundy's cousins, Sam Cowell, who was a deacon of the church, hid pornography in his house, which Bundy found and pored over as a toddler.

When Louise was twenty-two, still living at home in Philadelphia, "the baby that would one day become one of America's most infamous murderers began to grow within her," MacPherson wrote. "She was unwed and apparently never told anyone who the father was. . . . There was evidence that she was made to feel deep shame and had ample motivation to abhor this unborn, unwanted child."

Records obtained from a home for unwed mothers in Burlington, Vermont, show she left her home seven months pregnant in September 1946. She was accompanied not by a parent but by the local minister's wife. On November 24, Theodore Robert Cowell was born.

MacPherson reports that Louise left the baby in the Vermont home for three months (Bartsch had spent six months in his first "home"), then returned to take him back to her "depressed and ill mother and a thundering father." She stayed with her parents three years, than abruptly moved clear across the country to Tacoma, Washington. Evidently she felt it was not comfortable for her or her child to remain in her father's unhappy home.

The MacPherson article advances the original and startling suggestion that Bundy's father may have been Louise's father, that she was raped by her own parent. Bundy

was not told, until years later, that the man in whose house
he lived the first three years of his life was not his father
but his grandfather. As a child he was taught to call his
grandfather "Daddy" and his grandmother "Mommy." His
real mother was supposed to be his older sister.

Picture Bundy as a sensitive, bright child, believing that
his depressed grandmother was his mother, and his violent
grandfather, who hid pornographic books in the house, his
father. Little boys copy their fathers; he is the model for
the expression of both their violence and sexuality. Bundy
reported that as a three-year-old, he eagerly looked at the
nude bodies of beautiful women in the hidden pornography books. He was undoubtedly aroused both sexually and
aggressively too early in life—sexual and aggressive instincts are still fused at this age. With Bundy, they were to
remain fused instead of separating, as is normal, because
of the unspoken traumas, in his early life.

Bundy's great-aunt was quoted in the article as saying
of the family, who claimed Bundy was "adopted," that "I
knew things were not right. . . . I was smart enough to
know damn well they weren't adopting a baby. No adoption agency would give them one; Eleanor wasn't well
enough to take care of one! I knew it had to be Louise's
baby. But they wanted to cover up. All we ever got was
evasions. I had a very secretive brother. . . . No wonder
Ted has come to a tragic end. He was never told the facts.
Surely he had to catch the discrepancies."

MacPherson reports that when a family member once
asked the grandfather about Bundy's paternity, "Sam became enraged and apparently he acted like a madman. He
was wild. He was furious." Louise always denied her father was the child's father.

In Tacoma Louise met and married John Bundy, a hospital cook and very religious, as was she. He worked in a
Tacoma restaurant. MacPherson, who interviewed both,
describes Bundy as dominated by his wife. She often interrupted to finish the few sentences he offered. During the
interview she frowned when asked to described her father,

then said, "Well, he *could* get awfully mad and yell out. You could hear him from here down to the corner. He had a bad temper, but it wasn't . . . anything. He was never violent with anyone."

Then she revealed a key fact, one hidden for more than a decade of intense speculation over Bundy's background, MacPherson said. Louise admitted, "My dad *did* beat up on my mother once in a while."

If the child Bundy saw his supposed "father" attacking his supposed "mother" violently, we are not surprised that in turn, as a young man, he attacked women violently. He would copy as an adult the behavior of his "father," no matter how cruel. The bemused child controlled the adult Bundy no matter how educated and charming he became.

Many confused feelings contributed to Bundy's eventual emotional illness. The weird fantasies within the small boy when his supposed "sister" suddenly took him away from his home to live clear across the country, then married and bore four other children whose father he had to make peace with, must have been devastating. As far as he knew, he now had no real mother and father—he was an outsider, a complete outcast.

According to MacPherson, later psychological tests showed that in the first three years of life in Philadelphia, "something horrid happened to Bundy in that home where reality—the identity of his biological father, his grandfather's tirades, his grandmother's illness—was never acknowledged, let alone discussed."

Marilyn Feldman, who administered a battery of tests for Dr. Lewis in 1986, declared of Bundy, "Severe rejection experiences have seriously warped his personality development and led to deep denial or repression of any basic needs for affection. Severe early deprivation has led to a poor ability to relate to or understand other people."

His Aunt Julia contributed to a deeper understanding of little Ted in his Philadelphia days. She recalled that when she was fifteen, she woke one morning to see the little boy "secretly lifting up the covers and placing three butcher knives beside me." At the age of three he was planning to use knives against a woman lying in bed, dressed in her nightgown. We may conclude that he had seen his supposed (perhaps real?) "father" threaten his supposed "mother" (really his grandmother) or his daughter Louise (Bundy's real mother) with a knife as they lay in bed dressed in night wear.

Aunt Julia, ten years younger than her sister Louise, also reported of the little boy, "He just stood there and grinned. I shooed him out of the room and took the implements back down to the kitchen and told my mother about it. I remember thinking at the time that I was the only one who thought it was strange. Nobody did anything."

Ted had not been punished for wishing to use a knife on an attractive woman dressed scantily, so this would mean to the three-year-old Ted that his behavior had been accepted. At the age of three, Ted's sexual feelings just started to emerge—sex and violence closely allied.

Such "extraordinary bizarre behavior" in a young child, Dr. Lewis explained, "is seen to the best of my knowledge only in very seriously traumatized children who have either themselves been victims of extraordinary abuse or who have witnessed extreme violence among family members." She added that the grandfather "certainly sounds as if he were an extremely disturbed individual." It is accepted by psychoanalysts that not only are sexual and violent aggressive impulses merged early in the child's development but an early interest in guns, knives, and various instruments of torture and death is apparent in their fantasies, reading material, and sometimes in drawings.

With the three-year-old Ted, his anger and his sexual feelings went beyond fantasy—he actually carried three knives into the bedroom of an attractive girl of fifteen. And in later life it is estimated he used a knife on at least fifty young women. In each case of assault the victim was probably a stand-in for his youthful mother, the first woman to arouse him sexually, but also, according to MacPherson, a woman for whom he held "an anger so deep" that as a young adult he asked his great-uncle Jack, a college professor, to adopt him.

Dr. Lewis also said that when a youngster has been "horribly traumatized so that he or she cannot tolerate what he has witnessed or been part of, he tends to totally repress and to be unable to call it to mind. And I suspect that this is what happened." Bundy could act out his violent and sexual desires, but he could not remember how they felt when he was a small child and intensely aroused by them.

Louise's aunt, Virginia Bristol, had paid for Louise to resettle in Tacoma near her uncle, Jack Cowell. She took the fictitious name of Nelson and passed herself off as a divorcée. She soon met and married John Bundy. Ted later told friends that when he was five, he felt so jealous of his "new daddy" that he staged a temper tantrum, publicly wetting his pants to get even.

His mother admitted that he was never told anything about his biological father, that "Ted never had asked about the—the 'other man,' because he never heard about him or had seen him or anything. . . . It wasn't something we ever talked about."

MacPherson wrote that Bundy bitterly deduced from all the secrecy surrounding his birth that he was unwanted. He had been abandoned first in the Vermont home, the most crucial time for a baby to have a mother. Forever after, as MacPherson said, "a child of Ted's intelligence and imagination could have developed the most horrible scenario to fill in the blank of who his real father was."

Bundy told Utah State Prison psychologist A. L. Carlisle that he found his birth certificate when he was thirteen, marked "father unknown." He shrugged, said to Carlisle, "I had had a sixth sense . . . I didn't feel nauseous or tearful." Carlisle wondered if the words "nauseous" and "tearful" might not actually reflect his feelings. Bundy recalled that at ten he was taunted by a cousin who called him a "bastard." According to a later girlfriend, he was furious at his mother for leaving him open to such humiliation.

He had difficulty controlling his temper tantrums as he grew up. His anger no doubt increased as he saw two half brothers and two half sisters enter the world. Four new rivals for his mother's love and attention, rivals who could boast they had both a mother and a father. It is no wonder that, as he said, he became obsessed early in life with detective magazines holding gory pictures of sexually assaulted bodies. One of his many destructive fantasies, as he killed attractive young women, may have been that he was getting rid of his rival sisters after satisfying his sexual desires. Bartsch chose boys, Bundy chose girls.

MacPherson points out that Bundy's early bizarre behavior either went "unrecognized" or "untended" as he tried to create the facade of the perfect little boy, the appeasing adolescent, the rising star in Republican state politics. She said, "The dark side was so concealed that when he first became a murder suspect scores of friends— writers, politicians, teachers, lovers—said that there had to be some ghastly mistake."

She describes his "one terrible genius" as the ability to create "his mask of sanity; he was a robot chameleon, instinctively able to divine and display any facet of the charming shell his public desired." The "robot" quality appears to have been copied from his mother's attitude toward the world.

MacPherson quotes Swiss psychoanalyst Alice Miller, an expert on childhood and violence, as explaining that "the roots of adult violent behavior can be found in a level of parental cruelty invisible to the untrained eye." Children may be instilled with a sense of hate and helplessness because they are never allowed to acknowledge feelings of rage and rebellion.

MacPherson concludes that the clues to Bundy's startling number of serial murders point to his early years and his relationship to his mother. During Dr. Lewis's last moments with him, using relaxation techniques, she enabled him to recall buried emotions. He talked in an intense voice about how he felt unloved by his mother.

Though she insisted she loved him, Louise Bundy, according to MacPherson, was seen by some as expressing love for her late son in a "mechanical" and "hollow" way, in words "devoid of emotion." Richard W. Larsen, interviewing her for his book *Ted Bundy: The Deliberate Stranger,* wrote that "Ted's mother has had a bone-deep feeling for some time that her son might not be the All-American boy." A close observer of mother and son during the Bundy imprisonment commented, "There was something chilling about how cold she was. In many ways, she talked like Ted."

It is more likely that in many ways he talked like her, for the child develops by copying the parent. One time he caustically told a guard when mail arrived, "No letter from my 'beloved' mother."

Dr. Lewis, a professor of psychiatry at New York University's School of Medicine, was interviewed for an article by Robert Crum that appeared in the *New York University Magazine* in January 1990. He pointed out that for the past eighteen years Dr. Lewis has been searching for answers as to what drives someone to murder or commit a violent act. She has interviewed not only men on death row for their bloody crimes but violent juveniles, adults, and their families.

She concludes that those who commit violence suffer from a combination of a history of severe abuse and/or family violence during childhood, as well as a combination of "neuro-psychiatric vulnerabilities" shown in learning disabilities, psychotic behavior, abnormal electroencephalograms, or actual epilepsy. "Investigators have long been aware of a connection between abuse and violence," she says. Violent adolescents often become murderers.

In this article she describes Bundy's grandfather as "an extremely violent and frightening man." This was Bundy's model during the first three years of his life, the most important years in the life of a child. He later copied the man he called "Father" when he attacked women.

Crum describes Dr. Lewis as "exploring the caldrons" of childhood, referring to her many long interviews with murderers and violent adolescents. He says her main concern is that "people who are sick get treatment, not disposed of," referring to death row inmates scheduled for execution.

Dr. Lewis's description of the abuse some parents are capable of was described in studies she conducted with fifteen death row inmates in four states. One mother tied her son to a water heater and horsewhipped him. Another burned her son on the chest with a hot iron and tried to choke him. Two inmates as children were held outside the windows of cars by their parents as they sped down highways. Others were beaten on the head with two-by-fours, threatened with shotguns, injured with axes. Twelve in all were violently abused as children, suffering serious head injuries that resulted in neurological problems of varying severity.

Ann Rule's *The Stranger Beside Me* gives a fascinating account of her relationship with Bundy as, at first, she refused to believe that the young man who had become a close friend was the savage serial killer. She points out that Bundy's retinue of friends and companions was "always heavily weighted with women. Some loved him as a man. Some women, like myself, were drawn to his courtly manners, his little-boy quality, his seemingly genuine concern and thoughtfulness. Women were always Ted's comfort—and his curse.

"Because he could control women," she went on, "balance us carefully in the tightly structured world he had manufactured, we were important to him. We seemed to hold the solution to that dead hollow place inside him. He dangled us as puppets from a string, and when one of us did not react as he wanted, he was both outraged and confused."

On the other hand, Rule believed that men "were a

threat [to him]. The one man whom he felt he could emulate [his grandfather], the man whose genes and chromosomes dictated who he was, had been left behind." When Bundy told her for the first time about his illegitimate birth, she said she sensed that he seemed "to consider himself a changeling child, the progeny of royalty dumped by mistake on the doorstep of a blue-collar family. How he loved the thought of money and status, and how inadequate he felt when he found himself with women who were born to it."

She added, "Ted never really knew *who* he was supposed to be. . . . His feelings toward his mother were marked with a raging ambivalence. She had lied to him. She had robbed him of his real father, although rational consideration shows that she had no choice. But half of Ted was gone, and he spent the rest of his life trying to make up for that loss."

One wonders too if his childhood wish to knife his Aunt Julia as she lay in bed was not really displacement of his wish to knife his seductive mother, who probably lay in the same room with him, if not the same bed, during his first three years of life. He seemed to be showing, in his knife act with his Aunt Julia, the real act he would later commit on young women, but which was unconsciously directed at his mother. Psychologists warn parents to give a child his own room at birth to avoid prematurely arousing the child's violent and sexual feelings, which he will later not be able to control if they are felt too intensely early in life.

"Something in me snapped. I knew I couldn't handle it anymore," Bundy said on television just before he died. What was the "it" he could not handle? The horrors he had committed as a man and the horrors in his early life that caused him to commit the later ones.

The act of murder tells us not only of vengeance on the "other person," the victim, but against the murderer himself, says Dr. Arthur S. Liebeskind, psychoanalyst. The murderer "makes war on himself, on any vestige of humanness that may have survived in his life from infancy on," Dr. Liebeskind points out. "The humanness he once felt as an infant was met by his mother or father or both, with such rage that he learned to turn his own needs into the kind of warfare his parents waged against him. This early warfare destroyed any possibility he could later enjoy intimacy with anyone."

Dr. Liebeskind adds, "The murderer perceives his victim as embodying the aliveness denied to him. The victim represents life being led in the present. The murderer believes the victim's existence is an insult, an attack, an assault on him. The possibility of 'aliveness' needs to be destroyed lest it awaken the possibility of aliveness in himself and the early warfare to which he was exposed. He destroys his victim as though screaming to the world, 'See what was done to me!' "

The answer to why serial killers emerge is not a simple one. It requires deep awareness of the many terrors and rages the serial killer felt as a child. While one of us (H.S.) was vacationing in the summer of 1990 at his regular retreat in the Adirondack Mountains, he saw once again on the walls of his room the picture of an Indian Chief and the words underneath: "You do not judge a person until you've walked a mile in his shoes." This applies to the serial killer as well as all others.

Some serial killers murder only young women, as Bundy did. Others, like John Wayne Gacy of Des Plaines, Illinois, murder members of the same sex. Still others murder only children, as did Jürgen Bartsch. In *Serial Murder*, Ronald M. Holmes and James De Burger discuss the criminal activities of men who turn to serial murder.

Like mass murder and murder sprees, serial murder is not truly a new phenomenon, these authors say, although it occurred much less frequently in the early years of this nation, when crimes of passion and felony-related killings predominated. But there were occasional highly publicized serial murders in the first four decades of this century. A surge in multiple murders occurred in the 1950s, and serial killing soon became a focus of research and law enforcement efforts.

Holmes and De Burger ask, "Why does serial murder pose especially serious problems?" They answer,

> For one thing, it tears at the fundamental fabric of trust that permits a community to function adequately. Homicidal crimes of passion, though reprehensible, can at least be understood and dealt with rationally. Most adults can "understand" that volatile interpersonal relations sometimes end in a homicidal act. Even in felony homicides and "classical" murder, it is possible in a grim sort of fashion to make sense of the homicide in terms of the pattern of relations between the killer and the victim.
>
> But this cannot be said of serial killing where an innocent person is slain, sometimes after inhumane torture and degradation, by a stranger. And then there are the effects on survivors. Consider the gnawing uncertainty that families experience when a child or youth is abducted; the numbing grief when identification must be made of a battered body that once was a lively human being. These effects of serial killing simply cannot be fathomed by any form of research or analysis.

The type of serial killer called the "lust killer" does not stop at the fulfillment of sexual gratification as most rapists do, the authors say. Many such killers are sadistic, so that "the extent of their sexual pleasure depends on the amount of torture and mutilation they administer, and ultimately, on the killing of their victims."

The lust killer receives his sexual gratification from the use and abuse of others, whom he views as sexual objects. The authors report that Bundy told police officers Donald Patchen and Steve Bodiford in Pensacola, Florida, following the Chi-Omega sorority killings, "I'm as cold a motherfucker you've ever put your fucking eyes on. I don't give a shit about those people."

This is probably the way he thought as a small boy that his mother and her parents felt about him. Their disgust with and hatred of a "bastard" no doubt came through clearly as he slowly understood the emotional climate around him. He defended himself with the words "I don't give a shit about those people" and "I'm as cold a motherfucker you've ever put your fucking eyes on." Cold he was, cold enough to murder and mutilate the bodies of countless young women.

There are valid grounds for the point of view that the serial killer acts from a conscious perspective but is also influenced "by a variety of unconscious drives that are not as yet fully understood," the authors state. These unconscious factors "arise from myriad forces that we probably will never fully understand."

Dr. D. L. Carlisle, the Utah State Prison psychologist, who has almost daily contact with serial killers, believes they tend to possess a "multiple personality" structure. He sees the serial killer as driven by an overwhelming urge to kill. This urge, called by some serial killers their "beast" or "shadow," takes over to complete the murderous task when the urge to kill becomes unbearable to the conscious part of the mind.

"The beasts are visible only to the serial killers, who outwardly appear to be 'nice people,' " Dr. Carlisle explains. "But lurking just below the surface, with the serial killer aware of its existence, is the beast. With some of the serial killers, the person is no longer in charge, only the impulses of the beast." Only the wild, angry impulses of a child later unable to control his violent and sexual desires, as Bundy forecast when at the age of three he stood beside his aunt's bed with three knives.

Serial killers who have been interviewed say that in the midst of the killing they felt their personality had been taken over by a "beast." Some felt they were witness to the killing, helpless to stop it.

The first phase of "lust killing" is the fantasy of the kill itself. The serial killer spends much time thinking in advance and planning the crime. Fantasies played a large role in Bundy's behavior, influenced by the pornography and "true detective" magazines he collected, picturing violent and gruesome crimes.

The second phase of the serial murder entails the search for the "right victim." The victim must be someone who possesses certain physical characteristics or other features that attract the particular serial killer. We might guess that each young woman Bundy killed in some way resembled the women in his early life. He had a fetish for long hair parted in the middle of the forehead. Perhaps his mother, or Aunt Julia, had this kind of hairstyle. Or his sisters.

The third phase of the killing process is the display of an elaborate form of fantasy in which deviant sex and ritualism are featured. The act of murder itself is usually carried out through personal weapons—hands, fists, knives, hatchets, even the victim's underwear or stockings used for strangling. The killer often uses a ruse—tries to win the trust and confidence of the victim. John Wayne Gacy promised a job to entice young men into his home; Bundy often wore a cast on one arm and carried schoolbooks in the other to draw the sympathy of his intended victim. Other serial killers offered rides to hitchhikers.

For some lust murderers, an orgasm accompanies the moment of murder. Along with sexual release comes a surge of power and triumph accompanied by a feeling of completeness and wholeness, a feeling only short-lived.

Some serial killers believe each killing will be the last. But each murder will always fall short of its intended fulfillment. The compulsion emerges again and an attempt is made to regain the lost feeling of completeness, power, and sexual conquest.

Thus, the unconscious wishes buried in the mind of the serial murderer are never satisfied. Only when the early reasons for the fury of buried sensual desire and anger can be made conscious will the wish to kill and the terrifying feelings that accompany it be released in words, not acts.

The fourth and last phase involves the transportation of the body to a cellar or backyard, as in Gacy's case, or to a faraway "dump" site as in Bundy's choice. The serial murderer may also occasionally leave the body at the scene of the crime. These distinctions are important in helping investigators identify the type of serial killer.

Thomas Harris's novels *Red Dragon* and *The Silence of the Lambs* describe the intense rage in the bones of the serial killer—a rage that reflects the depths of emotional torture suffered in childhood. As the lives of real murderers show, there seems little doubt that murder starts in the cradle—that the wish to kill is inextricably connected to the murderous behavior of those who brought up the murderer.

In *For Your Own Good: Hidden Cruelty in Child-Rearing and the Roots of Violence,* Alice Miller describes childhood as the "breeding grounds of hatred." She points out that cruelty to a child can take a thousand forms and goes undetected even today "because the damage it does to the child and the ensuing consequences are still so little known."

The greatest cruelty inflicted on children, she says, "is to refuse to let them express their anger and suffering except at the risk of losing their parents' love and affection." The anger stemming from early childhood is stored in the unconscious, and since it basically represents a healthy, vital source of energy, an equal amount must be expended in order to repress it.

An upbringing that succeeds in sparing the parents at the expense of the child's vitality sometimes later leads to suicide or extreme drug addiction, a form of suicide, Miller explains. She speaks of "soul murder" of the child as the result of a parent's brutality, either sexual or physical or, in some cases, a complete lack of empathy for the child.

In one chapter, titled "Adolf Hitler's Childhood: From Hidden to Manifest Horror," she discusses the source of his deep hatred of the Jews, attributing it to a father who beat him regularly and who was believed to have had Jewish ancestors. As a boy, Hitler lived a life of "horror," Miller says, "beaten and demeaned" by his father every day from an early age on, frequently "unmercifully with a hippopotamus whip," then being held "against a tree by the back of his neck" until he lost consciousness.

The feelings of fear he repressed in childhood when his father's blows assailed his mind and body overtook him at the peak of his success in the form of nightmares, sudden and inescapable, when he would wake screaming, Miller points out. She adds, "Had he made the entire world his victim, he still would not have been able to banish his introjected father from his bedroom, for one's own unconscious cannot be destroyed by destroying the world."

Thus, the cruel man we might call the greatest serial killer of all time had a cruel father and a weak mother who could not stand up for her son. Miller sums up: "I have no doubt that behind every crime a personal tragedy lies hidden. If we were to investigate such events and their backgrounds more closely, we might be able to do more to prevent crimes than we do now with our indignation and our moralizing."

She used the example of Hitler, she said, to show that "even the worst criminal of all time was not born a criminal," that "those who persecute others are warding off knowledge of their own fate as victims." True emotional understanding of serial killers and others who commit murder "has nothing to do with cheap sentimental pity," she said. On the contrary, if we understand the reasons a murderer is driven to kill, we have a chance to greatly decrease the number of future murderers in the world.

The chapter on Hitler is followed by "Jürgen Bartsch: A Life Seen in Retrospect," as Miller describes the case mentioned at the start of this chapter. She praises Paul Moor for making the effort to understand Bartsch as a hu-

man being, to examine his childhood in "pathetic surroundings the very day he was born."

She said she also presented his story to show by means
of a concrete example "how the way a murder is committed can provide clues for understanding the soul murder
that occurred in childhood. The earlier this soul murder
took place, the more difficult it will be for the affected
person to grasp and the less it can be validated by memories and words."

Later, the only recourse is "acting out." "For this reason," she sums up, "if I want to understand the underlying
roots of delinquent behavior, I must direct my attention to
the child's earliest experiences."

She admits that despite her attentiveness to Bartsch's
life as described by Moor, as she underlined many of the
passages, she found she had overlooked the most important one—"It was the passage about Jürgen being beaten
as an infant." She added that the fact she had passed over
this passage, of the greatest importance in corroborating
her thesis, showed her how difficult it was to imagine an
infant being beaten by his mother, how difficult "not to
ward off the image of it but to let the full implication sink
in on an emotional level."

This explains, she said, why psychoanalysts are also "so
little concerned" with these facts and why the consequences of "this sort of childhood experience have
scarcely been investigated."

She concluded that she did not intend to assign guilt to
Bartsch's mother for going after him with a knife, or for
sensually bathing him until he was almost a man. She
added, "My very point is to refrain from moralizing and
only show cause and effect, namely, that those children
who are beaten will in turn give beatings, those who are
intimidated will be intimidating, those who are humiliated
will impose humiliation, and those whose souls are murdered will murder."

Perhaps it would have been the better part of wisdom to
have granted Theodore Bundy's request to stay alive and

permit a psychoanalyst to delve deeply into his warped mind and free the murderous fantasies of his earliest days of horror that drove him to kill an uncounted number of young women. We would then have strong proof of how the unbearable mental pain of childhood leads to the creation of an uncontrollable adult monster who seeks revenge on those who early crucified his soul.

This was poignantly pointed out in "The Genesis of Murder From Child Abuse," the title of an evocative lecture given by the late Flora Rheta Schreiber at Corpus Christi College, Oxford University, on November 19, 1984. Brett Kahr, the psychoanalyst who arranged for the lecture, introduced Schreiber as the author of *Sybil* and *The Shoemaker: Anatomy of a Psychotic,* discussed earlier.

Schreiber started her lecture by saying,

When you think of murder in cliché fashion you believe, They killed, so kill them. To hell with them. It is very rare that anyone takes a humanistic approach and thinks of the man or woman who killed as a human being who was born and lived and had reactions and feelings and aspirations and was human.

But when I began interviewing Joseph Kallinger I realized I had to understand a human being from the moment of conception—from foetus to felon, if you like. I found a human being of extraordinary sensitivity, of many insights and potentialities who had been raised by foster parents who abused him cruelly, both emotionally and physically. He was the victim of a psychosis from which his crimes were inseparable as a seemingly normal citizen became a criminal and committed three murders.

She said that "from the beginning of Kallinger's life, his adoptive parents denied the child his potentiality and humanity, his life forces. Denied childhood friends, or any kind of play, he grew up without love, without proper nurture until he became schizophrenic, living in his own un-real, vengeful world."

She concluded,

Nothing that happens is not connected with early childhood. It is illustrated by what Wordsworth meant when he said that the child was father to the man. A friend of mine said one day, "I was sympa-thetic with little Joe, I cried for him. But not for Joe the man." I pointed out to her, "They are one. The little boy is omnipresent throughout the adulthood. The inner child of the past accompanied the adult, the little boy's suffering moved and shaped the adult's acts."

Perhaps some day the power of the inner child of the past will be recognized, as we understand more about the deeply buried wishes to kill, not only in murderers but to some degree in all our hearts.

As Proust wrote, "There are a thousand selves in each of us." Many, if not most, of those thousand selves are terrified, vindictive, vicious, raging chil-dren who appear within the serial killer. But to lesser degrees those thousand selves exist in all of us and at times cause us to hate ourselves and those to whom we are close.

We tend to overlook the fact that we all have a Jo-seph Kallinger within, whom we try to hide and deny. That is why we are so helpless in coping with serial killers like Kallinger. We do not in the end want to confront ourselves. Among the "thousand selves" in us are the king, the queen, the Broadway star, and the sexually active lover. Most of us can ac-cept those selves but find it burdensome and abhor-rent to face the murderer who resides in us all.

9

Murder of the Self

"There is no refuge from confession but suicide; and suicide is confession."

—*Daniel Webster*

Barbara Watson began working for the Department of Parks and Recreation in Westport, Connecticut, in 1974. She was thirty-five years old, divorced, with two young children, both girls. Her salary was low but she somehow took care of her daughters. Her friends described her as a woman who never complained, was always cheerful, understanding, and helpful to others.

She brought up her children without any financial aid from her former husband and also looked after everyone around her—sick and elderly family members and friends, even people she barely knew. But it seemed no one took care of her, because at the age of fifty she killed herself.

Mrs. Watson was known as a "good neighbor" who baked cookies and cakes for others. She took her daughters to services in the church where they were confirmed and which she had attended since she was a child. Her minister, the Reverend Theodore Hoskins, recalled her as "Babs," a woman who "always had a big smile on her face."

At the Department of Parks, Mrs. Watson worked her

way up from clerk typist to office manager and eventually became a deputy director, a job she held until the last five years of her life.

"Her duties included collecting, reporting, and depositing revenues in all areas," said Stuart McCarthy, the Department of Parks director, who referred to her as "a likeable woman who would go out of her way at all times to be helpful."

Part of her duties was to collect greens fees at the municipal golf course. These were mostly paid to her in cash and it was this money that was to bring about her suicide.

The records of the rounds played on the course did not correspond to financial records for the revenues collected. McCarthy said, "It came about as a result of a casual conversation between myself and the golf course supervisors at a conference." There was an inquiry and the discrepancy was found to be large and long-standing. More than $30,000 a year was unaccounted for in each of the last three years, a total of $99,402.

"My feeling was we had discovered just a clerical error," McCarthy said. "Absolutely a clerical error. You've got to trust an employee who has been in that position for fifteen years. That's not a place you go looking for trouble."

To resolve the matter, he suspended Mrs. Watson, with pay, pending the outcome of the investigation. The suspension began on Monday, November 20, 1989, and on Thursday, November 23, Mrs. Watson ate Thanksgiving dinner with her family, whom she invited to her home. Her mother, a woman in her seventies, was in a nursing home in Fairfield.

On Thanksgiving she also stopped to visit an uncle, William Harding, eighty-six years old. Then, at 11:38 the next morning, Westport police responded to a call from a member of her family. Mrs. Watson had been found in the bedroom of her modest home, a plastic bag covering her head, dead of self-inflicted asphyxiation.

She left no note, and no one recalled her complaining of

financial problems. But both daughters were in college, one a senior at the University of Michigan, the other a freshman at a college in Rhode Island. It was likely, authorities thought, she had taken the money to pay for her daughters' college expenses. Family and friends felt shocked and deeply bereaved.

Each year, 45,000 persons in our country kill themselves. Barbara Watson's desperate act offers clues as to why they do. Their motives vary, but all self-murderers have much in common.

Through their suicide, people who kill themselves say, "I have given up hope that life offers any real pleasure." Though feelings of doom and misery can be precipitated by such misfortunes as a terminal disease or an illness that prevents a person from working, suicides take place as a rule because of serious psychological problems.

The suicidal person invariably hates himself and feels unable and unwilling to go on living. His self-esteem has been lowered to such a degree that he loathes himself almost consistently. While all those who hate themselves have, by definition, a limited self-esteem, the one who commits suicide lacks all hope of regaining a positive self-image. For example, the man or woman rejected by a lover or spouse may feel very suicidal. He believes life now holds no meaning unless he can be accepted once again by the one who has jilted him. Many a person who commits suicide feels there is no reason to live if the one he has loved ceases to love him, because his precarious self-esteem depends on this love.

Or a person who has a certain status—such as Senator, Congressman, or member of the social elite—may depend on this status for his self-image. If he loses this status, he may want to end his life.

When someone murders himself he may also be full of shame because something forbidden he has done may be exposed, or has been exposed. This is what happened to Barbara Watson. She worried that her embezzlement would be revealed to everyone. She hated herself for being known as a thief who might lose her job. This job status had become very important to her, and probably influenced deeply her wish to kill herself.

In understanding the low self-esteem that is part and parcel of the one who commits suicide, we have to keep in mind that self-image, body image, and how much a person likes himself have little to do with reality. When Marilyn Monroe killed herself by overdosing on pills, she was successful, beautiful, and esteemed by the world. She gave up hope because she viewed herself as a slut or tramp—a hated little girl, worth nothing.

Marilyn's suicide, like Barbara Watson's, suggests another characteristic of the self-murderer. The suicidal person experiences not only shame about an act being exposed, such as money stolen, but also a profound feeling of loss. Barbara Watson's loss was that of a job, status, affection, and income. What precipitated Marilyn Monroe's suicide was loss of a lover, Attorney General Robert Kennedy, who decided to remain with his wife and eight children instead of marrying her. She also feared, albeit not realistically, that she was growing old and losing her beauty—which would mean a loss of film roles and the admiration and income they would bring. Her self-worth was obviously predicated on her sense of feeling outcast from the day she was born.

Perhaps the least recognized dimension involved in the murder of the self is that the suicidal person is almost always in a rage. Nobody kills himself who has not intended to kill somebody else. But the suicidal person feels so guilty about his murderous wishes toward another person that, instead of becoming a murderer, he turns the angry wishes against himself and says, "I should die, not you, because I feel so hateful and unwanted."

Marilyn Monroe probably wanted to kill Robert Kennedy, but feeling hopeless, despairing, with limited self-esteem, and full of shame about her imagined physical decline (as the result of several operations on her beautiful body, including removal of the gallbladder, and miscarriages) she turned her rage on herself. Barbara Watson probably wanted to murder all those who were making her overwork, taking in money for their pleasurable games of golf, while she was feeling little sense of achievement.

The person who kills himself has just as much hate as the one who murders somebody else, but he has less hope than the murderer, lower self-esteem, and he feels more shame. He cannot allow himself the possibility of staying alive because he hates himself so deeply.

The rate of suicide in our contemporary culture has steadily risen, particularly for young people in their teens and twenties. In this group, at high risk for suicide are independent, noncomplaining, achievement-oriented souls unable to share their feelings of dependency and hopelessness even as they cannot cope with the overwhelming sense of isolation that accompanies their severely depressed state.

Unable to tolerate their vulnerabilities, they often prevent those close to them from recognizing their depression and proceed quietly to a well-planned suicide that, like Barbara Watson's and Marilyn Monroe's, stuns everyone they know. The victims have often put up a brave front for years, shielding feelings of low self-worth from the world.

There are two types of people who murder themselves. One is the man or woman reared in deprivation of all kinds but particularly emotional deprivation. These victims have had depressed or absent parents or parents who were cold and unloving. All the hatred a child feels toward such ungiving parents, he later turns against himself as he continues into adolescence and adulthood. He feels unloved all through life and unable to muster much self-approval. A child always believes that if his parents are emotionally or physically unavailable then he, the child, is despicable and unlovable.

The second type of person is surprisingly different from the first. He has received a great deal of success, love, and attention. But there is one hitch. He can love himself and feel worthwhile only if he is successful, if he is loved, and if he receives attention. The Hollywood star, the politician, or the successful writer such as Hemingway commits suicide when the success or the attention or love for which they yearn no longer is forthcoming.

They have never learned to take no for an answer. They cannot experience defeat with grace. They remain enraged if they do not get the attention and love they believe they deserve. They have come from homes where their parents loved them, ostensibly very deeply. The problem, however, was that their parents only loved them conditionally— when they were a success. This is hardly love. It is emotional blackmail.

Given this kind of "love," the child in growing up feels he can like himself only if he succeeds academically, athletically, or in other areas chosen by the parents. He falls into a rage because the love is so conditional. He wants unconsciously to murder his parents because they do not give their love to him for just "being."

As an adult, such a person thinks of himself as shameful if he does not satisfy others. If he fails at a task he attributes this to his unworthiness and is convinced he should be punished for a bad performance. Such need for punishment, if severe or distorted enough, may take the form of suicide.

Many men and women believe that in order to like themselves they have to go to great lengths to try to achieve what is sometimes the impossible. There are those who believe they must produce but cannot write the great American novel, or make a million dollars in the stock market, or be an actor or actress on Broadway. When they fail to reach their ambitious goals, they think of themselves as despicable, deserving only ostracism, scorn, hatred and perhaps death at their own hands. They possess an internal terror that will not diminish.

Most suicidal acts involve two persons. Although the drama takes place within the head of the person who kills himself, nearby stands someone who is very close—a spouse, a parent, a lover. Most suicides reveal the murder in their hearts directed at another person as they leave a note telling the accused guilty one (the man or woman they would have liked to murder) how very sorry they are that they have to resort to suicide.

The murder in the suicidal person comes through as punishment of the survivor, whom he indirectly accuses of causing his death. One rejected woman left a note for her lover saying, "I tried my best to get you to love me the way I desperately needed love. I realize it is too much to ask from you. Since I cannot live without you, I must depart from this uncaring world."

Such a letter has been written hundreds of thousands of times. It reveals the suicidal person's sadism, in which he accuses the lost lover of causing his death and tries to make him feel guilty and suffer.

Although much is known about the motives of the self-murderer, a number of misconceptions and myths exist about suicidal phenomena. It is often alleged that those who talk of suicide do not commit it. But of every hundred persons who will kill themselves, eighty have given strong warnings of their intentions. Studies reveal that the suicidal person furnishes many clues to his plans. He speaks of feeling dejected or depressed or mentions others who have committed suicide.

It is often assumed that suicidal persons are desperately intent on dying. Yet most suicidal men and woman are very conflicted about whether to live or die. They often gamble with death, leaving it to others to try to save them. Almost no one commits suicide without letting those who are close know how he feels. A man of twenty-five, planning to marry, received a "Dear John" letter from his fiancée. He became severely depressed and required hospitalization. He improved in the hospital, was released and felt better. Then, after dining with close friends, he went home and shot himself through the heart.

The difference between actual suicide and the suicidal gesture also has to be understood. The person who commits suicide has given up hope, lost all self-esteem, sees life ahead as unbearable, without any pleasures. Although a sense of hopelessness is rarely completely irrevocable, a number of persons who threaten to kill themselves never intend to. They take pills but not enough to cause their death. They slash their wrists but do not lose much blood. Or they jump out of a window only three floors from the ground, not incurring severe injuries.

The suicidal gesture is more common among women than men in that women attempt suicide three times as often as men, although men complete suicide three times as often as women. Although there is some evidence that the ratio for committed suicides seems to be changing, moving toward but not yet achieving an equal proportion between the sexes, the tendency still exists in women, more than men, to wish to be saved. Women in our culture are less conflicted about their dependency wishes. Consequently they often cry out for help, something men cannot do as openly.

The major characteristic of a suicidal man, woman, or adolescent is a very strict conscience, what psychologists call a "punitive superego." The suicidal person lives with a harsh evaluation of himself and, therefore, is always worried about how much punishment he deserves. The product either of a punitive family atmosphere or a parental love that was conditional, he cannot truly like himself because he never has been loved for himself. The love he received rested almost exclusively on how much he satisfied parental ambitions. Consequently, he feels he is always breaking some kind of invisible law and must be punished if in any way he defies a parental view, mandate, or wish.

Very often the suicidal person is so exasperated by having to "produce" for exacting or hateful parents, whose voices he still hears in his twenties, thirties, or later, that he stops living so he will no longer feel tormented beyond endurance. Many a suicide may be viewed as the person's way of defying the voices of parents who constantly berate him. As one suicidal person put it, "If I kill myself, I'll kill those voices that are always admonishing me."

The suicidal person feels very pressured and believes the cessation of living relieves the pressures. Often he has the fantasy that he will be loved in afterlife, perhaps forgiven for his real but more often imaginary crimes. Perhaps too he will be mourned by the parents or loved ones he feels have never loved him as much as he deserves.

The occurrence of one suicide almost always increases the number of suicides among family, peers, and friends. This is particularly true with teenagers and college students, as though suicide sometimes becomes like a dangerous, contagious disease.

This suggests that in all of us lies some wish to commit murder of the self. Probably everyone alive has thought of dying at his own hands during his lifetime. The wish to kill ourselves, like the wish to murder others, exists in all of us and may be ignited when we are close to others who kill themselves (adolescents seem to bear this out). Murders appear to increase after a murder is committed and the same seems to apply to suicide.

Parents may speak of suicide and stimulate the child to do the same. One daughter grew up hearing her mother often say to her three, at times obstreperous, children, "You'll be the death of me!" The daughter would then feel guilty at the thought that she might be responsible for her mother's suicide, and, because she experienced herself as such "a bad girl" often had to punish herself with her own suicidal thoughts.

Suicides occur in families for many reasons. First, men and women who marry each other are always quite similar emotionally even though they may be the last to admit this. A self-destructive man who hates himself will feel quite sympatico with a woman who hates herself. We know of the many suicide pacts that exist between husbands and wives and lovers. Just as two people who have a deep interest in music will find each other and want to be with each other, so too will two people who are self-demeaning find each other and want to spend time together.

Children use their parents as models without consciously realizing it and, therefore, if a son or daughter has noted a parent's self-hatred, or had a parent who committed suicide, the child will model himself after his parent's behavior. Just as sons and daughters with parents who are divorced will choose divorce as their later solution to an unhappy marriage, children who have seen suicide in their home or heard threats of it, may be more inclined to commit suicide.

Every family has its rules and regulations for coping with conflict, which govern the behavior of the whole family. Usually these rules and regulations are unconscious and rarely articulated. A rule that exists in some families is "When things go bad, stop living," whereas another family may prescribe, "When things go bad, persist and struggle."

Just as we have emphasized that murderous wishes exist in all of us and that the difference between an actual murderer and the rest of us who occasionally think about murder is only a matter of degree, so, too, the same applies to suicide. While only a small percentage of our population commits suicide each year, many exist in a depressed and masochistic condition.

Thousands of people are severely depressed, but their depression remains unrecognized and they are regarded instead as chronic underachievers, fatigued men and women, hypochondriacs, and sufferers from physical problems. Depression is a universal phenomenon we all know from time to time. No one is exempt from sadness, temporary loss of self-esteem, dislike of the self. But in contrast to the suicidal person, most of us eventually find something or somebody to help restore our self-esteem and increase our belief in ourselves.

It is important to understand some of the reasons why we become depressed so we can help ourselves lessen the depression and return to more positive feelings of self-esteem. The depressed person feels angry because of some blow to his ego. If it is important to be loved and admired for certain attributes and these attributes are demeaned or derogated, we may feel depressed unless we acknowledge our anger at the person who demeans us. We should also recognize that we are not despicable and deserve to die because someone does not love us the way we would like to be loved.

Depression also exists when we feel we have lost somebody or something essential. Part of living invariably brings losses we have to make peace with in some way. We lose friends, family members, jobs, lovers, status. Many of us feel depressed because of these losses instead of accepting them as "necessary losses," as Viorst puts it. We also find it difficult to hate those who have left us through death or other circumstances. Consequently, we turn the hatred on ourselves instead of hating those who have in some way frustrated us.

In contrast to depression, in which we feel sadness, loss, and low self-esteem, masochism is a much more complex but also more universal phenomenon. In masochism we undergo physical or emotional pain in order to feel pleasure. The masochistic person feels he is not entitled to pleasure. His conscience, or the voices of his "internalized" parents, forbid enjoyment of life. He must suffer while receiving pleasure, before the pleasure, or following the pleasure.

One extreme of masochism exists when people are whipped or physically hurt during sex. Many married couples believe that sex is more enjoyable after an argument in which feelings were hurt. Thinking we are punished, sexual pleasure now seems more permissible. Marriage counselors have noted that many couples argue *after* enjoyable sex—punishing themselves later for the pleasure they have received but do not feel entitled to enjoy.

When gripped by severe consciences, we seek penalties and punishments. Failure in careers, unhappiness in marriage, and the disappointments of life seem to relate to our over-exacting consciences, which constantly tell us that unless we behave like upright, conforming, nonsexual, nonaggressive children, we should be punished. The characters created by Dostoyevski and Tolstoy frequently burden themselves with pain and misery in a fervent desire to expiate their sins.

Just as suicides and murders are two-person events, masochistic behavior is also meant to be seen by another person. Often the masochist suffers silently but hopes his suffering will be admired. He may turn the other cheek in hurt and pain but yearn for applause as he does so. The masochist is an angry exhibitionist, constantly crying out, "Love me because I suffer." This is not too far removed from the emotional state of the suicidal person who begs, "I've suffered so much, remember me in my death."

There exists in every masochist a martyrdom, an eagerness to sacrifice himself. This martyrdom is aimed at a cherished but also hated person—a spouse, a mother, a father, a child, a friend. The masochist, because he needs to suffer, will stay saddled for years with a grumbling boss, a torturing spouse, ungrateful children, or a faithless lover.

The same characteristic unrecognized in the suicidal person and the depressed person is present in the masochistic person—he is at heart a sadist, as pointed out earlier. He cannot acknowledge the fact, but portrays himself as the opposite of a sadist, though he is secretly sadistic in his thoughts.

As Theodor Reik in *Masochism in Modern Man* said so poignantly, describing the masochist, "The lambskin he wears hides a wolf. His yielding includes defiance, his submissiveness opposition. Beneath his softness there is hardness; behind his obsequiousness, rebellion is concealed."

The masochist, Reik further points out, "enjoys suffering, as Don Quixote enjoyed his defeats—for his lady's sake. In the most sublimated form of masochistic character an abstract ideal takes the place of the desired woman.

Thus Saint Francis gladly suffered for the sake of his beloved Lady Poverty." Reik also says that the masochist gains a victory through defeat. By suffering, he wins a battle in that he hopes to make his tormenter suffer and painfully rue his cruelty.

There is surprisingly little in the scientific literature to show that self-destruction is part of the psychology of everyday life and not confined to the extreme of suicidal acts. Although scientists have been remiss in showing how all of us at times are our own worst enemies, many writers, poets, and dramatists of centuries past have provided a rich understanding of the many aspects of self-hatred. They have demonstrated how intimately linked self-esteem and self-hatred are.

Injury to our narcissism loosens our aggression. This always leads to murderous thoughts and occasionally to murderous acts. But most of us tend all too frequently to turn hatred on ourselves. William Congreve observed two hundred years before Freud that a woman's narcissism when hurt could turn to menace. He wrote these famous words in *The Mourning Bride:*

> *Heav'n hath no rage like love to hatred turned.*
> *Nor hell a fury, like a woman scorned.*

Dr. Greogry Rochlin in *Man's Aggression: The Defense of the Self,* referring to this quote from Congreve, remarked, "But to the present the exceeding vulnerability of a woman's narcissism and its relation to her aggression and her tendency then to turn it on herself remain more in the poet's lines than in the clinician's research."

In sum, we are all born with an aggressive drive. When we are frustrated in any way we may use our aggression in either hostile thoughts or hostile acts. In its extreme form hostile activity is murder.

Aggression can be healthy and constructive if used for love, work, art, or other forms of self-assertiveness. But if our hostile thoughts or murderous wishes are totally unacceptable we may turn them on ourselves. Like murder, self-hatred takes various forms—its extreme is suicide, its lesser extremes are depression and masochism.

Our normal aggression exists to be used constructively, and this includes healthy self-criticism and "taking the blame" when we are wrong. There is a difference in feeling depressed and not knowing why, and the ability to take a look at the realistic reasons we may feel temporarily unhappy, masochistic, or suicidal. Again, it is a question of the depth of our feelings, all of which are normal and natural to some degree.

PART 5

Taming the Murderer Within

10

Understanding the Murder in Our Hearts

"The death penalty serves one main purpose—it is a vehicle for our revenge."

—*Jack Levin*

A black box over his handcuffs keeps the inmate from picking the locks. Chains lead through the box, padlocked around his waist. Shackles hobble his feet. Three guards surround him as he walks slowly down the hall from the cell block to the visiting room.

Each guard carries a yard-long black stick made of sturdy plastic, tipped with steel bearings. "Rib-spreaders," a guard explains. "We use them as prods. They separate the ribs without breaking them."

This is the scene at the United States Penitentiary in Marion, Illinois. While more rigid in its discipline than most prisons, it is nonetheless similar to other prisons that lodge murderers and perpetrators of violent crimes. Many a murderer spends twenty-two hours a day in solitary confinement.

Because incarceration in prison seems our society's way of coping with overt murderers, our state prison systems are now more overcrowded than ever. As the rate of murder keeps accelerating, the number of prisons increases along with the number of prisoners.

As society becomes alarmed with the increase in crime and drugs, a prison industry that already consumes more than $13 billion a year is showing no sign of recession. While most experts agree that new prisons alone will never solve the problem of increased homicides, incarceration continues to be our society's major way of coping with the murder scene.

As one of our foremost experts on crime and particularly murderous crime, Dr. Karl Menninger, wrote, "Our prisons are places where people who can't make it on the outside are detained without being rehabilitated. Prison shouldn't be a place where men are broken, embittered and further dehumanized. Being criminal to a criminal is committing a crime."

While there are a few who support Dr. Menninger's point of view, most societies believe that murderers are not to be understood or rehabilitated but isolated and punished severely. The atmosphere of many prisons is quite murderous. This is true not only in the United States but in most prisons of the world.

Recently an Egyptian human rights group charged that torture and sexual abuse of prisoners had become so widespread that such treatment "now appears to be a matter of policy by security forces" holding those detained both for political and nonpolitical reasons.

Throughout the world we find, particularly in dealing with murderers, that the personnel use whips, electric prods, and electric shock treatment, applying them to sensitive parts of the suspect's body. They also use water hoses to extract confessions of guilt for behavior not permitted in the prison.

Incapacitating a murderer is a goal of criminal law that primarily serves the public. It does not serve the offender except insofar as it prevents him from committing acts that may lead to his restriction in even more hurtful ways. Using incapacitation seems the best way we have devised to deal with murderers. There has been little attempt to understand the motives of the murderer and what possibilities exist for rehabilitation. Our basic belief is that if we punish the offender severely enough he may be deterred from wrongdoing in the future.

There is however much controversy in the field of criminal justice as to the value of punishment as a deterrent to murder or other crimes. In recent years some social scientists have presented a theory in which offenders are considered rational people who weigh the risks and benefits involved in committing an antisocial act and can be helped to mend their murderous ways if they receive a helpful hand from society, not a punitive one.

The actual data on the effectiveness of imprisonment as a deterrent today are far from conclusive. The high rates of recidivism following imprisonment do not show that imprisonment has diminished the future criminal behavior of most offenders. In fact, it appears that the incarceration itself, where the prisoner is subjected to a sadism that borders on torture from his fellow prisoners and sometimes even from the guards, makes him feel even more murderous when he leaves prison than when he entered.

This sadistic treatment of our prisoners, particularly those who commit murder and other violent crimes, is often more barbaric than the treatment the murderer experienced in growing up, where his murderous feelings were first activated.

Just as there is no proof that the crime of homicide may be deterred by long sentences in prison, there is no proof that the death penalty deters it either. Yet almost 80 percent of all Americans now favor the death penalty, and the remaining 20 percent would be willing to make an exception if it meant eliminating the Ted Bundys.

According to a recent survey conducted for ABC News and the *Washington Report,* the reason underlying Americans' overwhelming support of executions is usually revenge. We believe the most serious crimes deserve the most serious punishment, as we recall the statement from the Old Testament, "An eye for an eye, a tooth for a tooth," the retaliation principle.

When we hear about a murderer, rarely do we want to understand what drove him to murder; more often we wish to kill him. It is difficult to understand that the vengefulness we feel toward a murderer, which drives us to champion execution, is identical to the wish for revenge the murderer feels for what he believes to be the horrendous injustices in his life.

Our desire to tame the heart of a murderer is quite limited. We feel as murderous toward them as they do toward those they have killed. We wish either to kill or torture them. This makes a murderer, if he is imprisoned, even more murderous. Just as the murderer's murder accomplishes nothing, so too the death penalty has not in any way decreased murder.

Jack Levin, Professor of sociology at Northeastern University in Boston, author of *Mass Murder: America's Growing Menace,* concluded from his massive research that the death penalty serves one main purpose—it is a vehicle for our revenge. He points out that the arguments for the death penalty are almost always emotionally charged. Many believe that convicted killers "deserve to die," that "getting even" is valuable as a measure of psychological compensation for the victims and society.

Why should we spend hard-earned taxpayers' money to imprison a murderer when we could just as easily execute him at much lower cost? Frequently overlooked is the fact that the fixed cost of running a maximum security prison is little affected by the presence of a few additional inmates serving long sentences for murder. The warden and guards have to be paid and the heat maintained.

Moreover, because of the lengthy appeals process required by the Supreme Court in capital cases, it costs much less to imprison a killer than to execute him. In Florida the average cost of a case that results in execution is $3.2 million, whereas the estimated cost of imprisonment for forty years runs about $500,000.

Many argue, "If it costs so much to carry out the appeals process, then take the prisoner back and string him up!" Often lost in this argument is the number of errors made in the use of the death penalty. Since 1900, according to Levin, 139 men and women have been sent to their death, although later proven innocent. As a nation we should feel deep guilt at learning this. Once in a while an accused but innocent murderer has been set free when he has been able to get help in proving he did not commit the killing.

The death penalty, Levin shows, has little if any effect on decreasing the murder rate. He quotes a study by Dan Archer and Rosemary Gantner of fourteen nations in which the death penalty was abolished and the murder rate went *down*. In Finland, they reported, the homicide rate dropped 59 percent; in Italy, 30 percent; in Sweden, 63 percent; and in Switzerland, 46 percent.

Even more ironically, research conducted by the criminologist William Bowers suggests that the murder rate actually *rises* for a period of time after a killer has been executed, as it produces what Bowers calls "a brutalization." It appears that would-be murderers identify more with the executioner than the inmate. Similarly, the homicide rate goes up for three days after a heavyweight boxing fight in which potential sadists identify with the victorious boxer.

While it is true that capital punishment protects society by guaranteeing that certain killers like Ted Bundy will never kill again, when we sanction murder through the death penalty we endorse more murders. Just as war creates an increase in homicide rates because it sanctions killing, the death penalty appears to produce the same effect. It would seem that a life sentence without the possibility of parole would probably lessen the number of potential murderers.

We need to study far more carefully the degree of vengefulness we feel toward those who commit murder, for this probably influences the punitive way we treat murderers. Revenge usually begets revenge—the effect the death penalty seems to possess.

* * *

The argument that rehabilitation of a murderer is unrealistic remains far from proven. Those who have attempted it have not been too successful, though it has never been tried on a large or thorough scale. We do not think of murderers as human beings who are extremely emotionally disturbed because of a lack of care and love in their very early lives, which usually have been full of violence.

Instead of subjecting murderers to further sadistic treatment, sometimes bordering on torture, in the prison environment, we might think of offering them the chance to understand why they felt murderous, to face the fear and rage of their childhood and master the trauma that drove them to murder.

Many think that finding the manpower to turn our prisons into rehabilitative institutions is a naive quest, inasmuch as it has never been done in America or in many other parts of the world. It *is* a dream—but a dream that could be realized if a society recognized that hatred helps no one but that caring, understanding, and love enrich our lives. This is a truth that most mental health workers attest to with deep conviction.

When a community becomes upset about the hatred in its midst, it acts. The rape of the Central Park jogger in New York made many question whether young men from broken families living in poverty could be rehabilitated. A dramatic increase in other vicious crimes throughout our nation has caused more and more politicians and community activists to begin to recognize that something different must be done if we are to cope with this all-time high level of murder and violence.

When alcoholism was recognized as a disease, time and money were found to try to arrest it. Thousands of paraprofessionals and professionals were mobilized to aid the victims. Possibly college students and graduates could be trained to understand the distorted mind of the violent person and empathize with such a mind enough to help him. Recently policemen and correction officials have been obtaining the help necessary to understand rather than become enraged at the violent man, woman and child.

As in the case of Willie James Bosket, Jr., imprisoned for life in New York State, the murderer is usually raised in a sordid atmosphere that increased his violent feelings. He responded to sadism with sadism, perpetuated a vicious cycle that thousands of others also contributed to, increasing our rate of homicide and the number of prisons and prisoners.

In his moving book *The Prince of Tides,* Pat Conroy has his hero Tom Wingo say, while talking to his psychoanalyst friend Susan Lowenstein, "There's only one thing difficult about being a man, Doctor. Only one thing. They don't teach us how to love. It's a secret they keep from us. We spend our whole lives trying to get someone to teach us how to do it and we never find out how."

Many believe we should try to rehabilitate more prisoners, including murderers. Instead of treating the murderer murderously, we should assess him psychologically and try, for the first time in our history as a nation, to rehabilitate him.

This means a reduction in society's intense murderous response of revenge—a heavy demand on us but not impossible to fulfill if we can become more understanding of our own murderous responses to the murderer.

In addition to Dr. Karl Menninger, who cried out for years for the humane treatment of killers, another spokesperson was Anna Freud. She asked that psychoanalysts approach criminals and delinquents with the assumption that their acts against the law be understood as the outcome of a set of distorted beliefs acquired in childhood.

Referring to her interviews with and observations of criminals, she wrote,

> In many of the instances scrutinized, one feels that the commitment of the actual criminal act is unnecessary, almost fortuitous, i.e., that there is usually a moment when the sequence of events could have

been altered and deflected decisively by comparatively minor intervention. That is, the tension which finds its outlet in the criminal act could have been reduced through human or therapeutic contact. . . . This view might drastically reduce the actual commitment of acts that have to be brought before a court.

She went on to say,

This hypothesis rests on the assumption that there is actually in a large number of cases such a point at which the constellation within the individual is not only favorable for intervention but also where there are manifest signs to betray this possibility. If this is true, a new system of "crime prevention" could be based on it, comparable to the existing schemes for the detection of the earliest signs of cancer and tuberculosis.

Anna Freud pointed out that the potential murderer and other potential criminals often reveal certain types of behavior prior to the killing. She said we could deter many crimes if society, including parents, spouses, employers, friends, were more attuned to the unusual way the potential murderer thinks and behaves. Further research should be carried out to develop a clearer picture of how the potential murderer suffers emotionally in childhood, but we have given many clues throughout this book.

We know the potential murderer is very preoccupied with himself, frequently shows an inability to express a wide range of human feelings, often feels extremely angry and hostile but masks his hostility by withdrawal or, in some cases, by excessive feigned kindness.

We also know the potential murderer is deprived emotionally, socially, and pyschologically. Members of minorities such as blacks and Hispanics, often subjected to deprivation, are more apt to be murderers. But sometimes those like John Hinckley, who are brought up in luxurious surroundings but in some way lack consistent, loving parenting, also reveal their potential as murderers.

We could spend far more time trying to understand why a man kills, conduct further experimentation on how to help him face and conquer the feelings and fantasies that have driven him to murder, if we spent less time and money on legal issues involving the death penalty and on punitive incarcerations.

Another way to reduce murder in our society is to help policemen and other law officers behave less murderously with the accused. Police brutality occurs to some extent in all our major cities. During a six-week period in Houston, two police officers shot and killed several motorists after stopping them for traffic violations. Two other policemen were found guilty in rape cases, one arrested for heroin possession, one charged with coercing sex from a prostitute, one reassigned amid charges of police harassment, and the homes of two searched as part of a drug investigation.

These charges caused heated debate. Some citizens maintained that the incidents exposed pockets of police corruption and racism, but top officials described the acts as symptoms of budget cutbacks and low morale. It is interesting that police officers involved in violent or murderous behavior speak of economic deprivation and psychological depression. Assuming they are correct in this assessment of their violence, such understanding of themselves could be used in their work with violent adolescents and adults.

A psychologist and former policeman, Dr. Harvey Schlossberg, with co-author Lucy Freeman, wrote *Psychologist With Gun,* which later became a television series. Schlossberg drew on his experience with the New York City Police Department to describe methods he found effective in treating the violent law-enforcement officer. He applied group principles and psychotherapeutic procedures to produce long-lasting gains. If his procedures worked with violent policemen, there is every reason to believe they can work with other violent individuals. We might question whether policemen who murder unnecessarily or use sadistic force to cope with their inner tensions are much different from violent prisoners.

As implied throughout this book, the feel of violence is everywhere—it pervades our culture. Much rage and potentially murderous feelings may arise in the workplace. Psychologists and other mental health experts recognize that those unhappy with their jobs sometimes use the work situation to act out sadism, violence, and occasionally murder. A man who has been let go will return to the office and shoot not only the one who fired him but everyone in sight.

Many children are whipped and brutalized by unhappy, overwhelmed teachers. Many patients in hospitals, particularly mental hospitals, are treated savagely by unhappy, overworked doctors, nurses, and other personnel. Many members of the armed forces have been sadistically brutalized in recent years by their superiors. In a number of instances, they lost their lives because they were placed in torturous situations—forced to do endless pushups, made to go without food for days, feeling more helpless than primitive man in the wild.

While direct murder does take place occasionally within labor unions and in schools and offices, the more subtle type of murder can be seen every day—an emotional or "soul murder" in which complete contempt is expressed by those in control as they berate someone they feel is inferior. Physicians have sexually abused patients, and, as mentioned earlier, child-care workers have abused their innocent, vulnerable charges.

Many persons are miserable on their jobs and feel furious at their colleagues, bosses, clients, or patients. While it is true that we may bring to the workplace the anger we feel toward spouses and children, it is also true that when we are not respected, when our sensitivities and vulnerabilities are not considered, when our strengths are not appreciated, we may become quite violent.

Another area in which we display fury is in the world of sports. Why is there so much violence in sports, a violence obviously appealing to millions who look forward eagerly to watching their team destroy another team as if it were a fight to the death? An athletic event is much like a war. The excitement that takes place is similar to that of battle. Bands play, patriotic songs are sung, and prayers are said at the start of the game.

We cannot expect to win all the time, for what we call "reality" inevitably holds deep disappointments, even for those who reach the top of the ladder. But in sports both players and fans fervently make a large investment in winning, as the yearly athletic forays get under way in baseball, football, basketball, tennis and golf. The players compete directly, the fans vicariously, as both avenge themselves for past hurts and discharge the hatred and murderous fantasies they have endured many times in life when they felt like losers.

Vengeance, revenge, hatred—all are sanctioned in the world of sports. The loser is humiliated, the winner extolled. One woman, an ardent Mets fan, asked herself one evening after the Mets had lost a game to the Pirates, a team they usually conquered, "Why do I feel so miserable at this loss? What does a baseball game mean to me personally that I sink into a depression because the Mets don't win?"

She was in therapy and asked her therapist this question. A Mets fan himself, he was well aware that he felt slightly down when they lost. He answered, "You identify with the team, you play along with them, hoping to defeat the enemy—your parents of childhood and your siblings."

"Is that good?" she inquired.

He laughed. "It isn't good or bad. It just *is*. Millions of people feel the same way. It's a natural outlet for the release of some of our angry feelings."

"Do I always *have* to be a winner?" she asked.

He said reassuringly, "We all want to be a winner. This is part of being human."

Winning and losing, with all the intense emotions attached to these feelings, are by definition part of most sports, so that from time to time we even see members of the same team at war with one another. In 1989 Daryl Strawberry, a million-dollar outfielder on the Mets, discharged some of his murderous, competitive outrage on the captain of his team, Keith Hernandez. Strawberry suddenly struck Hernandez in the face during spring training when Hernandez told him to "grow up." It is obvious that many hidden feelings exist among players on the same team in the warlike atmosphere of many sports.

Fans become as depressed or as elated as players and they do not forget their feelings over the years. Ask a Brooklyn Dodger fan how he feels thirty years after the Dodgers deserted him to live clear across the country and he will exclaim, "Kill the bums!"

To win, for a fan, means to be like the competent, strong, capable, and potent player with whom the fan identifies closely. To lose means the fan sees himself as humiliated and weakened—essentially a good-for-nothing, as he feels the player is, weak and impotent. To win means unconsciously that he has overcome the power of the "gods" of childhood—superior parents and powerful siblings. Many an athlete says in effect after a loss, "I'm finished, I feel dead," meaning he has been murdered, at least in spirit.

The degree of our identification with the aggressive athlete has not been fully appreciated by those involved in sports as player or fan. As a fan, the closer we feel to an athlete we admire, following him or her through the season, the more we are involved in the fantasy of killing or being killed.

Actress Robin Givens was recently quoted in *Penthouse* as saying of her ex-husband, heavyweight champion Mike Tyson, "I loved the danger ... He was exciting. I think that what people don't realize with a certain type of woman is that there are times when she wants the man she is with to be . . . a man. Michael told me that he was going to kill me and that the world would be grateful because he's made them think that I'm bad."

Givens's statement informs us that a violent man may be very attractive to some women. It also tells us she enjoyed taking part in a battle, that not only was she a fan of her husband but in her day-to-day marital encounters enjoyed the threat of violence as "exciting."

Givens no doubt enjoyed the situation of being near a man who made his living assaulting and weakening his opponents. Just as many ancient societies extolled the victorious warrior with the words "To the victor belongs the spoils," we extol athletes who conquer others. Women love them, men envy them.

Many a fan says with a smile, "I feel much less depressed since my team won today," the opposite of the woman who told her therapist she could not understand why she felt so depressed after her team lost. When a team wins, to many a fan this means, "I have won a war," as he identifies with the star of the game or with the winning team.

While our "hate culture" has to be redirected if we are to tame the rage in our hearts, we recognize that this prescription seems both idealistic and fanciful. But we are more optimistic about the possibility of helping people understand their hatred than changing the political arena, the work arena, and other segments of society that are cruel and hurt innocent people.

Those who harbor hatred and show their violence have been helped in various forms of psychotherapy—individual therapy, group therapy, family therapy—and the results have been very encouraging when they recognize that violence is a means of coping with vulnerability and desperation. It is much easier to help someone suffering in this way than it is to convince a politician or a bureaucrat that hatred and violence are not constructive for people, when they are reaping some of the benefits of hatred, for example, during a war or in a racist or sexist workplace.

Mental health experts have not yet been successful in showing society that a "love culture" is a productive culture and a loving person is a happy, achieving one. Understanding the murder in our own hearts requires a more mature perspective on all the relationships we have examined in this book—whether personal, political, or military.

With regard to our children, we need to recognize what many psychologists and historians have shown quite conclusively: while we are less openly murderous toward our children than our predecessors were, we are far more ambivalent and hypocritical. Contemporary adults, both parents and some professionals, are constantly of two minds in their dealings with the young and their ambivalence takes many forms.

For example, there is growing resistance among young adults to bring up a child and a decided trend toward the postponement of childbearing. More and more children are turned over to the care of others and, consequently, miss out on much-needed parenting, which they cannot help but resent.

Child psychiatrist Dr. E. James Anthony, who has studied this phenomenon carefully, states, "The manifest reason given for not wanting [children], our not wanting to take care of them, is the desire for self-fulfillment. But a deeper analysis often reveals an unresolved ambivalence originating from the would-be parents' earliest experiences. Therefore, there is much to suggest that a core of ambivalence is fairly widespread in the adult-child relationship of our time and culture."

In discussing marital relationships, we pointed out how hatred and violence are often par for the course of marriage. Men and women find it difficult to empathize with each other, cooperate with each other, nurture each other. We believe that to tame hatred in marriage, the partners have to recognize and tame their own childish wishes to be parented and learn to accept a certain amount of frustration, as well as willing to give more of themselves, instead of demanding more from their partner.

Violence and hatred exist in marriage because spouses demand more than is reasonable from each other in their attempt to constantly gratify their infantile wishes. When adults unconsciously wish to regress to being a child, they will hate their mate for not making this possible. Physical and/or verbal abuse predominates, and the children become deleteriously affected.

In the area of work, men and women have to be treated more humanely. The rage and murderous wishes often activated in the workplace emerge when we are treated impersonally and without respect. Rage becomes most intense when members of the work force feel like machines and their unique wishes, hopes, and desires for recognition are overlooked or scorned.

The understanding of the self we all hide inside to some degree is not easy to achieve, but if we delve deeper and deeper, we will find the reward high as murderous feelings slowly ebb away.

The term "soul murder," mentioned earlier, was first used in 1832 to describe the case of Kaspar Hauser, a seventeen-year-old boy who had been confined for his entire life in a cellar, cut off from all communication with the outside world. He seemed curiously devoid of emotion; he appeared to feel no anger at the man who had cruelly jailed him and no astonishment when he was suddenly set free. With the care of a few understanding persons, he began to display a capacity for learning, but then regressed and wound up as an obsessive-compulsive automaton. His early tragic life was too harsh to be undone. To spend his first seventeen years in a cellar, loved by no one, had been too severe to enable him to recover.

Later in the nineteenth century, the playwrights Strindberg and Ibsen used the term soul (or psychic) murder to describe the process by which a person's capacity for love and joy was destroyed. Dr. Leonard Shengold, in his *Soul Murder; The Effects of Childhood Abuse and Deprivation,* described it as "neither a diagnosis nor a condition. It is a dramatic term for circumstances that eventuate in crime—the deliberate attempt to eradicate or compromise the separate identity of another person. The victims of soul murder remain in large part possessed by another, their souls in bondage to someone else."

Soul murder can result from sexual or violent abuse in childhood, or from deprivation of communication, deep nurturing, or love. Sometimes the child will turn into an actual murderer who goes his early tormentor one better. Or the child can become psychotic, feel brainwashed, spend the rest of his life in mental institutions.

Soul murder is most prevalent among minority groups such as blacks, who have experienced much deprivation and limited support from cohesive families and a sympathetic community. Many blacks in the United States still feel like slaves "in bondage to someone else."

Kierkegaard said, "Life can be understood only by looking backward. But it must be lived looking forward." To understand ("looking backward") our very early wishes and fantasies about the murder in our hearts enables us to "look forward." Some may need help from therapists before they gain the emotional strength to delve into what they believe is the grim past. Others are strong enough to do this by themselves. Still others find the reading of books helps one to know the self better.

Whatever the method, the act of understanding the self more deeply results in easing the wish to murder in our hearts. This releases the psychic energy formerly used to hold back conscious awareness of both the forbidden wish and the pain. We can now put that energy into building a far happier life.

We can reduce the murder in our hearts if we face an obvious truth. This truth holds that love is far more beneficial to our lives than hatred.

Hatred erodes our souls and our bodies and is rarely satisfying except for a few angry moments. Constant hatred and murderous fantasies, when not understood and mastered, lead to depression, somatic ills, poor performance on the job, and unhappiness in marriage and the family.

How do we tame the murder in our hearts so our lives can be more enjoyable and fulfilling?

As noted several times, prolonged feelings of violence and murderous hatred mean that the child within feels deprived, threatened, and vulnerable. Most of those governed by murderous feelings chase rainbows, try to gratify impossible childish wishes. They still strive for continued bliss, for the Garden of Eden or the lost paradise they believe can be regained.

Most of us want what we want when we want it. Then, like infants, we despise those who do not supply us with the perfect paradise, the perfect job, the perfect orgasm.

When we human beings (who so often act inhuman) can accept the fact we all are infants in a part of our mind and heart, and identify the rainbows we all chase as we search for the impossible, then we will become less hateful toward our spouse, parents, children, colleagues, and friends.

While we all need to like ourselves in order to function with pleasure, we are apt to feel hateful if we continue seeking the impossible. Few are likely to be billionaires or Hollywood stars, supermen or superwomen. As we have shown, many of the "successful," such as Marilyn Monroe and Ernest Hemingway, have felt so miserable they committed suicide.

Many of us are like children who cannot share, who rage at the siblings they believe receive more love. We all hate to take no for an answer, but life can be more enjoyable if we are able to accept a no, rather than feel outraged. We cannot always be the center of attention, admiration and love but must face the fact that others may resent us at times or compete with us unfairly even when we have done nothing to warrant their dislike. The mature person who enjoys life, who can love and be creative, recognizes that others may hate him for unjust reasons and accepts this as part of life. As some baseball philosopher once said, "You can't win 'em all."

One of the difficulties many of us face, mentioned several times, is that we do not differentiate between normal, healthy aggression and hostility and hatred. We should allow ourselves irritation and anger when we feel frustrated or deprived. It is unrealistic to smile when someone steps on our toes, literally or figuratively. But if we believe we should be a perpetual prince or princess, we will only hate our frustrators and seek revenge indefinitely, perhaps harboring it to the day we die.

One of the major contributors to immature hatred and violence is the wish for revenge. Murderous battles in war, politics, marriage, and elsewhere involve revenge in which a person or group "gets even" for being mistreated. When this wish is strong, we are usually reenacting a childhood experience that should have been understood and mastered.

Most marital fights, lovers' quarrels, power struggles in work and supposed friendships are reenactments of ancient family traumas that never were put to rest. One man found himself constantly criticizing everything his wife did, from cooking and cleaning to making love. His hatred toward her diminished as he realized he was getting even with his exacting mother of childhood.

A young woman curbed her indignation at her fiancé after she accepted that confronting him with his passivity was part of the unresolved battles with her father, who "didn't make me his one and only when I was a child."

Rage toward friends and colleagues frequently reenacts battles with brothers and sisters, who we all tend to feel had it far better than we did (in some instances, they actually *did*). To like ourselves as adults and live constructively, at some point we have to say, "That's the way it was. No on can change the past. But I can have a happier future if I understand this and feel more of a person in my own right."

Often we ascribe to others the feelings of hate and wish

to murder that we have never faced and thus cannot tolerate consciously. We tend to degrade minorities—those who in one way or another are not in life's mainstream. If we could accept the psychological truism that there exists a boy and a girl in everyone, we would not be so contemptuous of gay men and lesbian women, on whom we project the buried feelings we cannot accept in ourselves.

"Knowledge is power," wrote the philosopher Francis Bacon. Not the knowledge of the outside world but of the world within the self that constitutes the true power. If we know ourselves and our fantasies, wishes, and fears, we will choose a mate who knows himself fairly well. We will no longer blame others for the unpleasant, frustrating moments that occur in our life. We will be able to tolerate our own and other people's mistakes and to ask them to tolerate ours. We will not expect a mate to be perfect—the one fantasy that dooms a marriage more than any other.

Sharing—true sharing from the heart—does not come easy. Watch a baby: he wants it all—his mother's total love, affection, and care. As siblings we pretend to share, to love each other, but at first it is difficult to accept the rival, for we now believe the love of our parents for us is far less.

The more hatred a child feels within the family as he grows up, the more he will wish to kill. The more sexual abuse there is of young boys and girls, the more we find later sex crimes committed by the ones who were abused or watched the abuse.

We live with a new kind of war in this country, one in which irresponsible, violent, depressed, and angry men, women, adolescents, and children daily destroy their lives or the lives of others. Drugs—chiefly crack and cocaine—have brought the murder rate to an alarming high. In the first six months of 1990, one thousand men, women, and children were killed on the streets of New York City, and the national murder rate was up 18 percent.

A policeman commented, "There are three shootings in

half an hour in New York. It's as if we were in the middle of a war zone. A whole generation of kids are lost to this murderous act."

An addict of eighteen said, as he held up a young woman and demanded her money, "If I have to kill you to get the next hit, I will." One commentator who referred to crack as "the call of the wild," said of the United States, "It's like the night of the living dead."

Perhaps one of the best ways to tame the murder in our hearts is to accept what the twentieth-century pioneer psychoanalyst Harry Stack Sullivan wrote: "We are all more human than otherwise."

Being human means that to some degree we are all murderers in the inner core of our being. But by becoming aware of our murderous wishes we can assure ourselves of far happier lives ahead. If we can accept the fact that those who commit murder are angrier than we are because of what they suffered as children, we will begin to empathize more with what are called "the less fortunate."

We will hate less, be it our marital partner or a murderer in prison. We will enjoy life more in this imperfect universe—a universe that will become safer and friendlier if the hatred among its occupants can turn more toward friendship and caring. But most important is the ability to look within the self and know all of us feel hatred when we are wounded in any way by someone we love.

"Love looks not with the eyes, but with the mind," Shakespeare wrote. It is our mind that brings the awareness we are all capable of hatred at times and we must not demand perfection of ourselves and others.

Rather we should seek acceptance of the self and others despite our human imperfections. We should recognize that there is no Garden of Eden on earth, nor any paradise that can be regained.

When we can accept that the world is composed of vulnerable human beings who are quite similar, our understanding and empathy toward the murderer in our midst increases and the hatred in our hearts diminishes.

In the 1960s our youth kept clamoring, "Give peace a chance!" Perhaps for the 1990s, we should say, "Give love a chance!"

Epilogue

What has happened to some of the murderers described in this book? As of this writing, Joseph Kallinger is still trying to starve himself to death in Farview Prison, Pennsylvania. Theodore Bundy was electrocuted January 24, 1989, in Florida.

Paul Moor, who wrote the story of Jürgen Bartsch's life, was in New York City in 1976 when he received a telegram from a female German journalist who knew he would be interested in the news that Bartsch had died at twenty-nine years of age in a very dramatic way in the West German Prison Hospital. After eleven years in prison, he was given the choice of accepting castration and freedom or a life sentence behind bars. He chose castration. He died of heart failure two hours following the operation.

Soon afterward, Moor left New York for Mississippi to visit his mother. There he found a letter Bartsch had written just before the castration in which he said in Latin, writing in capital letters, *"Morituri Te Salutant!"* Translated, this means, "We who are about to die salute you." It was as though Bartsch knew he would not survive the operation.

The doctor went on trial not only for Bartsch's death but for that of a female prisoner who had died a week earlier, after he operated on her. The doctor was found guilty of administering thirteen times the amount of anesthesia needed for the operation; this is what killed Bartsch and the woman.

The murderous parents in this country discussed in earlier chapters are serving long prison sentences, in some cases for life. The murderous children have been incarcerated for ten and twenty-year terms.

With the possible exception of John Hinckley, currently in a mental hospital, none of the murderers were or are being helped to understand themselves and learn what drove them to kill. None have been given the chance to master their hatred and most, if not all, continue to live feeling worthless to themselves and to society.

It seems deplorable that we have made such little progress in understanding the murderer in our midst and the murder in all our hearts. Perhaps this is one important reason why the rate of overt murders continues to escalate and why marriages of hate, vengeful parent-child relations, and the incidence of suicide among teenagers continue to proliferate. Just as we isolate and do not wish to understand the Kallingers and the Bundys, the child beaters and the rapists, we tend to do the same with our own hateful and violent wishes—we do not want to deal with them.

If we can accept the murder in our hearts that seeks discharge because the child within us who wants instant gratification can't have it, we will become more accepting of ourselves and more loving toward others.

All of us wish to be loved all of the time and to be famous and rich most of the time. We find it difficult to accept reality with its restraints, frustrations, discouragements, and unfairness. The one who murders has experienced more emotional hardships and deprivations than the rest of us, but he is more like us than different.

Repressing and denying our hatred instead of facing it and exploring its roots leads to depression, masochism, and even suicide. Hatred, if never confronted, emerges in work, play, marriage—virtually everywhere in our lives.

As we are able to face our hatred and understand the clamoring child within rather than condemn him, we will respect ourselves and others more. Murderous feelings diminish when self-understanding starts. We will then truly wish to help others, even our prisoners, lessen the murderous wishes in their hearts.

Dr. Herbert Strean is a nationally known psychotherapist with over thirty years' experience. Lucy Freeman's previous books include *Fight Against Fears, The Beloved Prison,* and, with Dr. Strean, *The Severed Soul.* Dr. Strean practices, and Ms. Freeman lives, in New York City.

Compelling True Crime Thrillers
From Avon Books

BADGE OF BETRAYAL
by Joe Cantlupe and Lisa Petrillo

76009-6/$4.99 US/$5.99 Can

GUN FOR HIRE:
THE SOLDIER OF FORTUNE KILLINGS
by Clifford L. Linedecker

76204-8/$4.99 US/$5.99 Can

LOSS OF INNOCENCE:
A TRUE STORY OF JUVENILE MURDER
by Eric J. Adams   75987-X/$4.95 US/$5.95 Can

RUBOUTS: MOB MURDERS IN AMERICA
by Richard Monaco and Lionel Bascom

75938-1/$4.50 US/$5.50 Can

GOOMBATA:
THE IMPROBABLE RISE AND FALL OF
JOHN GOTTI AND HIS GANG
by John Cummings and Ernest Volkman

71487-6/$4.99 US/$5.99 Can

The Best in Biographies from Avon Books

IT'S ALWAYS SOMETHING
by Gilda Radner   71072-2/$5.95 US/$6.95 Can

JACK NICHOLSON: THE UNAUTHORIZED BIOGRAPHY *by Barbara and Scott Siegel*
                                     76341-9/$4.50 US/$5.50 Can

STILL TALKING
by Joan Rivers   71992-4/$5.99 US/$6.99 Can

CARY GRANT: THE LONELY HEART
by Charles Higham and Roy Moseley
                                     71099-9/$5.99 US/$6.99 Can

I, TINA
by Tina Turner with Kurt Loder
                                     70097-2/$4.95 US/$5.95 Can

ONE MORE TIME
by Carol Burnett   70449-8/$4.95 US/$5.95 Can

PATTY HEARST: HER OWN STORY
by Patricia Campbell Hearst with Alvin Moscow
                                     70651-2/$4.50 US/$5.95 Can

SPIKE LEE
by Alex Patterson   76994-8/$4.99 US/$5.99 Can